The Complete Disaster Home Preparation Guide

Robert A. Roskind

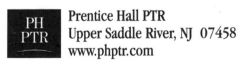

Prentice Hall PTR
Upper Saddle River, NJ 07458
www.phptr.com

ISBN 0-13-085900-1

90000

Library of Congress Cataloging-in-Publication Date

Roskind, Robert.
  The complete disaster home preparation guide / Robert A. Roskind
    p. cm.
  Includes bibliographical references and index.
  ISBN 0-13-085900-1
  1. Emergency management. 2. Survival skills. 3. Disasters. I. Title.

HV551.2.R67 1999
613.6'9--dc21   99-058693

Editorial/Production Supervision: *MetroVoice Publishing Services*
Acquisitions Editor: *Jeffrey Pepper*
Editorial Assistant: *Linda Ramagnano*
Buyer: *Maura Goldstaub*
Art Director: *Gail Cocker-Bogusz*
Cover Design: *Talar Agasyan*
Cover Design Direction: *Jerry Votta*
Project Coordinator: *Anne Trowbridge*

 © 2000 Prentice Hall PTR
Prentice-Hall, Inc.
Upper Saddle River, NJ 07458

Prentice Hall books are widely used by corporations and government agencies for training, marketing, and resale.

The publisher offers discounts on this book when ordered in bulk quantities. For more information, contact Corporate Sales Department, Phone: 800-382-3419; FAX: 201-236-7141; E-mail (Internet): corpsales@prenhall.com

All rights reserved. No part of this book may be reproduced, in any form or by any means, without permission in writing from the publisher.

All product names mentioned herein are the trademarks of their respective owners.

Printed in the United States of America

10 9 8 7 6 5 4 3 2 1

ISBN 0-13-085900-1

Prentice-Hall International (UK) Limited, *London*
Prentice-Hall of Australia Pty. Limited, *Sydney*
Prentice-Hall Canada Inc., *Toronto*
Prentice-Hall Hispanoamericana, S.A., *Mexico*
Prentice-Hall of India Private Limited, *New Delhi*
Prentice-Hall of Japan, Inc., *Tokyo*
Pearson Education Asia Pte. Ltd.
Editora Prentice-Hall do Brasil, Ltda., *Rio de Janeiro*

To James Talmage Stevens and Y2K, who together convinced me that preparedness is a lifestyle, not a luxury.

CONTENTS

PREFACE

I am writing this preface in the fall of 1999. My editor just called and said we need this soon. So I'm sitting here thinking what I can say to you, my reader, that will motivate you to really get prepared for any disasters that might happen in your area.

It is a strange time to be writing about preparedness. Though the need for preparedness has never been more obviously clear, complacency seems to still rule the day. This year Hurricane Floyd left thousands homeless on the East Coast of the U.S., Taiwan was hit by a major earthquake, and India just got their worst flooding in 100 years. This year computer viruses have crippled companies, the government is warning about possible cyberterrorism, and Y2K is looming like a specter at the feast. The reasons to prepare seem compelling. But the stock market is booming, holidays are around the corner, and there are over 100 channels on TV. Preparedness just is not part of this society's mindset. It is just more difficult to think of hard times during good times.

So what can I say to you to convince you that you should spend the time, energy, and money to be fully prepared for any natural or man-made disaster that may occur? Only this: If a disaster befalls you and your family, preparedness will be one of the wisest, most mature decisions you ever made. If none befall you, it will still be.

—*Robert Roskind*

THE BASICS OF DISASTER PREPAREDNESS

"Failure to prepare is preparing to fail."

—Benjamin Franklin

HOW TO USE THIS BOOK

This book has two primary objectives. The first part of the book will show you how to prepare your home so that you and your family can live as nearly to normal as possible after a disaster has interrupted essential services, such as water, electricity, or sewer. This first section will show you how to become more self-reliant no matter what the disaster, whether natural or man-made. This section examines preparedness as a lifestyle—always being ready no matter what happens. It is relevant to everyone, no matter what type of disasters occur in your area.

In the second reference section of the book are details about recognizing, preparing, and surviving individual disasters. This section discusses each type of disaster and what you need to know to prepare and survive. This section examines preparedness for an event. Preparation for the following disasters are discussed in this reference section:

- Earthquakes
- Floods
- Hurricanes
- Tornadoes
- Volcano eruptions
- Winter storms
- Nuclear emergencies
- Hazardous material accidents
- Thunderstorms & lightning
- Wildfires
- Landslides
- Tsunamis

In addition, several specific issues are also discussed, including:

- Disasters and people with disabilities
- Disasters and children
- Disasters and pets
- Fire hazards after a disaster
- Family disaster plan
- Family disaster supplies kit

WHY PREPAREDNESS?

Except in communities that have experienced previous disasters, preparedness is seldom done in most homes. There are many reasons for this. We feel it could never happen to us. It can be costly and time consuming. We hope the government emergency agencies will handle all our needs. We plan to but just never get around to it. And on and on. Though there are many reasons not to prepare, there is one compelling reason to prepare: if disaster hits, proper preparation can make the difference in terms of your comfort, your health, and preservation of your property and perhaps your life. Ask anyone who has been through disaster.

As we enter the new millennium, the reasons to practice preparedness are more compelling than ever; Y2K has shown this. The infrastructure we have built—the utilities, transportation, telecommunications, etc.—have become so huge as to be inherently unstable. A tree limb fell on a electric line in Idaho recently and knocked out power to several western states.

In many areas these systems are stretched to their maximum limit. A heat wave in the East Coast in early summer of 1999 caused hundreds of thousands to lose power due to overtaxing the grid. Natural disasters, hackers, terrorists, computer bugs, etc., can quickly bring these systems down.

In addition, the American Red Cross is predicting that we are entering a period of mega-storms, worse than we have ever seen. The tornadoes in the spring of 1999 created the highest winds (318 mph) ever recorded. There have been more deadly earthquakes in the last decade than in the previous hundred years. El Niño and La Niña are disturbing weather patterns.

Sen. Robert Bennett (R-Utah) recently stated that war in the future may include war on the Internet as enemy hackers attempt to disrupt vital computer systems. Weapons of mass destruction are becoming smaller while their availability on the open market is increasing. "Super computer bugs" are being created and released on the Internet that can bring down computers all over the world in hours. In early 1999 two computer viruses were released on the Internet that corrupted files and overloaded e-mail systems in computers worldwide. We have entered a period of technological vulnerability.

In addition to these trends, another parallel trend has occurred. As societies become more urban and suburban, they lose all control of creating what they need for their own survival. We no longer grow our own food, chop our own wood, draw our own water, etc. Because of this we have become more and more reliant on our governments to provide for us. We have become less self-reliant than earlier generations, who would never assume that the government would take care of them after a disaster. We are learning that our leaders and governments often do not have our best interests at heart.

This is a dangerous trend. Waiting for someone to take care of you after a disaster is quite different than being able to take care of yourself. The difference could cost you your home, your health, or your life. It is possible that disasters will begin to occur that will outstrip the capabilities of normal emergency agencies. We need to return to a greater sense of self-reliance, especially where disaster survival and recovery is concerned. We have entered a period of modern life where everyone should be constantly prepared to fend for themselves in the event of an infrastructure breakdown.

Preparedness as a Lifestyle

Disaster preparedness can be seen as preparing for a specific event or as a lifestyle. Most people when they think of disaster preparation, they think of getting ready for an impending disaster, say a flood or hurricane. This is disaster preparedness as an *event*. However, disaster preparedness as a *lifestyle* means being able to live as nearly normal as possible no matter what happens. This means preparing your home to be able to function in the event of an infrastructure breakdown that continues for an extended period of time.

A major question is how long should you prepare to function for a break in essential services and food delivery. The Red Cross recommends several days to several weeks. FEMA, until recently, recommended 2 weeks. I recommend a minimum of 1 month, with 6–12 being preferred. If budget is not a big issue, prepare for the high side. If it is, prepare for as long as is financially feasible. It may not be that those who prepared will eat while others starve, but rather that they may have more choices as to what they eat and more convenience in getting their food. Those who prepared may be able to stay home while others need to go to a shelter or relatives, or they may be able to shower when others sponge bathe.

You cannot get very far in the preparation process before you begin to realize that no matter how completely and cleverly you plan for your family's needs, all it takes is a few relatives, friends, or neighbors—who didn't prepare—to show up on your doorstep and collapse those well laid out plans. Of course your option is to remind them that you encouraged them to prepare, slam the door in their face and send them away cold or hungry.

If things get too bad, every one of us may need to make those kind of decisions. There may be just too many people in need. However, if the breakdown is moderate or slight (the most likely scenario), though we can't help everyone, we might be able to help some. It may be best to decide to prepare not only for your family's needs but for several others—if you can afford to.

Disaster Preparedness and Sustainability

As we begin to look at preparedness as a lifestyle, we can expand this concept to include more than just disaster issues. There is more and more compelling evidence that we need to change the way we are using our resources and our planet. We have created a hole in the ozone layer and intense El Niños. Our population growth alone is straining our systems. It took 123 years to go from 1 to 2 billion but only 11 years to go from 5 to 6 billion.

Consider this: In the last 24 hours,

- 200,000 acres of rain forest have been destroyed
- 13,000,000 tons of toxic chemicals have been released into the environment
- 45,000 people have died of starvation
- 130 plant or animal species have become extinct
- 432,000 tons of topsoil were lost

(From *The Last Hours Of Ancient Sunlight* by Thom
Hartman/Mythical Books, 1999)

Clearly we must begin to pollute less and use our available resources more efficiently. Our technology has outgrown our wisdom and we must catch up. Though as individuals we cannot solve all these problems, we can begin to adjust our own lifestyles to help. As we begin our disaster preparedness we will find that many of the changes or preparations we would make to prepare for a disaster are the same we might make to live more sustainably on the earth.

Some of these changes could include:

- Solar power
- Wind power
- Solar hot water heaters
- Solar battery chargers
- Solar ovens
- Composting (waterless) toilets

- Growing our own organic food with non-hybrid seeds
- Waste water recycling
- Fuel-efficient vehicles
- Recycling
- Low meat diet (most rain forests are destroyed to grow cattle)

All of these above methods not only pollute less and conserve more, but in the event of a break in the infrastructure, allow us a much greater degree of self-reliance. A family with composting toilets, solar power, water recycling, and vegetable and fruit gardens is much more able to operate normally if essential services are not available. Soon we must further develop, and eventually convert to, our decentralized, non-polluting sources of energy (wind, solar, wave, hydro, etc.). There is less than 50 years of fossil fuel left, and their use is destroying the environment.

A lesson these threats and disasters may teach is that we must cooperate, as individuals, as businesses, as countries, as a world. The competitive, enemy-thinking paradigm that has existed on this planet for generations must diminish and give way to a more compassionate one, or imminent disaster will catch us. This may serve to remind us that we are all interconnected and interdependent. As Martin Luther King, Jr. said: "The choice is no longer between violence and non-violence but rather between non-violence and non-existence."

FOOD AND HOW TO STORE IT

"It's my understanding that many cities still only have a 72-hour supply of food within their borders."
— Senator Gordon Smitt (R-OR) February 1999

THE PROBLEM

There is a growing concern that infrastructure failures could cause disruption of the food supply to your local supermarkets. This could make food limited and/or expensive. Most food is inventoried and distributed through a long supply chain. For example, when you buy a quart of milk, the grocery store computer tracks this sale and automatically sends reorders to their main office and on to the main distribution center and then on to the wholesale supplier. From there, this order is delivered to the dairy manufacturer and then over to a trucking company—all by computer. Keep in mind, most supermarkets only have a three-day inventory.

Much of our food must be shipped from hundreds or thousands of miles away. This means our, and our trading partner's, transportation system must be functioning effectively. Over 40% of our fruits and vegetables come from South American countries.

It may seem ludicrous that a country like the United States could have a food shortage. We can almost understand food shortages in other countries (in some areas of Russia people no longer greet each other with "Hello" but with "Do you have food?"). Here we have such an abundance of everything and large grocery stores are a testament to our food abundance. Remember, in three days—fewer if people get scared—shelves could be empty.

THE SOLUTIONS

In the event of a possible disruption of the infrastructure (power, water, transportation, etc.), we recommend a minimum of 4 to 8 weeks' supply of food be stored. However, with the possibility of a longer disruption, higher prices, or greater inconvenience in obtaining food, you may want to consider 6 to 12 months of food supplies.

There are two main approaches to food storage:

- Storing nonperishable foods that you normally eat
- Storing dehydrated and freeze-dried foods

Your In-home Grocery Store: Storing Nonperishable Foods That You Normally Eat

Perhaps the least disruptive and most palatable approach is to simply increase your normal supplies in your pantry. For instance, you may now have a week supplies of canned and packaged foods in your pantry. If you want to store enough food for 3 months, just increase your supplies and increase your storage space as needed. Then each week or two, just replace the food you have eaten, always eating the oldest food first. Most foods off the grocery shelf have a 6- to 24-month shelf life (see "Food Shelf-life Recommendations" at the end of this chapter). If you constantly eat from your pantry and "rotate" the food, it will never be out of date. Another advantage of this system is if disaster does not create food shortages, the food you've stored won't go to waste. You just won't have to shop as often after the event (Figure 2.1).

Figure 2.1   This pantry is stocked with all off-the-shelf grocery items. This food should last four people several months.

You may want to include the nonperishable versions of foods that are often stored in the refrigerator or freezer, such as canned and non-perishable meats (some canned hams need no refrigeration and are good for 2 years), canned and powdered milk, etc. Also be sure to include treats and sweets (cookies, candy, gum, chips, etc.) as these are always appreciated in times of increased stress (Figure 2.2).

The advantage to this approach is that it allows you to eat in a near-normal manner during any disruption, and should you decide to no longer store the food, you can eat it as you normally would. Think of your home, apartment, or other safe storage space as your personal in-home grocery store. Imagine having supplies of food and other necessary items on hand from which you can draw continuously for up to a year. Imagine everything in constant stock rotation—items consumed are replaced periodically and new items added as they are

Figure 2.2   Almost all grocery items have a one year+ shelf life. Many are good for several years.

discovered and enjoyed. Think about having quality foodstuffs to prepare wholesome and nourishing meals, very similar to the meals you are accustomed to eating.

There are several disadvantages to this approach. Because off-the-shelf grocery items are not dehydrated (though you can buy a few dehydrated products, such as potatoes, from the grocery store), they contain water and weigh more and take up more space. They are often not as nutritious as dehydrated or freeze-dried foods. Their shelf life is 12–24 months compared to the 10 to 20 years of their dehydrated or freeze-dried cousins. Grocery items have a broader selection than the other options and will cost less than freeze-dried foods and the same or more than dehydrated.

Planning for 4 to 8 weeks' supply of food takes time, thought, and money. Planning for a 6–12 month supply of food takes a lot of planning, thought, and money. It should start with a family meeting of everyone who will be eating the food to decide what you really want to store. Listen to everyone, as each person has different eating habits; stressful times are not the time to force eating preferences on anyone.

Purchasing canned and non-perishable foods in volume should not be viewed as shopping in greater volume at the corner grocery store. Considerable money and time can be saved by purchasing from discount price clubs, such as Sam's Club, Price Club, etc. Also, many food wholesalers that sell to restaurants, hospitals, colleges, etc., will sell to the public. They usually require a minimum dollar amount paid in full when you get the food. Many of these companies will even deliver to your house. Check your local yellow pages under "Food Wholesalers."

BUILDING YOUR IN-HOME GROCERY STORE

The important thing is to keep it simple. You don't need to go out and buy unfamiliar food to prepare an emergency food supply. So, in other words, you don't need to do anything weird. If you like tuna, just buy more of it. You can use regular canned foods like canned tuna, soups, fruit, vegetables, dry mixes, and other foods that you normally use. Other things to include could be pastas and grains. Buy foods that your family will enjoy but are high in nutrition. Also, canned foods don't require cooking, water, or any special preparation.

Just remember, you want to store foods that require no refrigeration and minimum preparation or cooking. Other nonperishable foods can include crackers, fruit bars, granola bars, bouillon cubes, peanut butter, trail mix, tea bags, coffee, and powdered milk. Be sure baking items require no eggs unless you plan to have powered eggs stored. You can buy powered milk in airtight containers which prevents oxidation. Typically, we don't give this a lot of thought but realize that much of the food at the grocery store that you buy everyday has a year shelf life or more, so you are really okay with a lot of the things you're used to.

Also get a good supply of dried beans, peas, rice, wheat, etc. These can be bought in bulk and are inexpensive, easy to store, and nutritious. If you are getting whole wheat, be sure you have a quality hand-operated grinder.

Also get a good supply of sprouting seeds (alfalfa, adzuki, lentils, mung, peas, triticale, wheat, etc.). Get organic beans from your health food stores. Sprouts, being a live food, are an excellent source of vitamins and minerals. Sprouts contain enzymes that aid in digestion, as well as needed protein, vitamins, and minerals. It's like having a garden in your kitchen. Seeds are small and easily stored until you sprout them. You can sprout easily at home and if you don't know how, your health food store probably has a pamphlet or book. This is perhaps

Figure 2.3 Sprouts, easy to store and full of vitamins and minerals, are perhaps the best stored foods.

the best of all stored foods (Figure 2.3). (Note: Recently ecoli and sal-monella has been found in raw sprouts. To kill these pathogens soak sprouting seeds in a mixture of one quart water and 1.5 tablespoons of unscented bleach for 5 minutes.)

Stock up on spices, too. Food need not taste bad just because you are operating in a disaster mode. Also, keep an extra supply of multivita-mins and other nutritional supplements around. The idea is to keep everyone's spirits up, so you don't want just a bunch of canned tuna and oatmeal. Be sure to get some enjoyable snack food and treats too, like chips, cookies, and candy. In fact, familiar foods are important in times of stress and disaster. This helps keep morale strong and lessens tension and anxiety. You also may want to consider purchasing a food dehydrator to dry your own fruits and vegetables. You can even make your own jerky. But remember, an electric dehydrator may not be usable if the power is down. There are also many books available on canning, curing, and smoking that you can look into.

Keep in mind any special dietary needs such as food for infants or the elderly. Nursing babies may need liquid formula in case they are unable to nurse. Canned dietetic foods, juices, and soups may be helpful for the ill and elderly. Whatever you do, don't forget pet food! They're completely dependent on us.

As you build up your inventory, you always want to rotate your foods, so you are constantly using and replacing your foods until you can't anymore. Try to use your foods when they are freshest; even canned goods gradually deteriorate. So rotate, rotate, rotate.

The best thing to do is to mark and date your foods so that you always know which foods to use at any given time. The best way to do it is to color code your foods according to the "Use by" date stamp, not the date you purchased it since different types of foods have different "use by" dates. Most nonperishable grocery store goods will last one year, but you still want to rotate as much as you can. However, often the "use by" date is in a code that you may not be able to decipher. In this case you may need to mark it according to when you purchased the item.

You can use different colored markers or get different colored paper dots at any stationary store (Figure 2.4). Then, create a color chart and

Figure 2.4   Put colored dots on each product. Each color should represent a different "use by" month.

allocate a different color to a different "use by" or "purchased" month. So, say January is blue; put a blue dot on all the foods you have that should be used by January, a green dot for February, a red dot for March, etc. Or you can have different areas of the pantry shelves set aside for the different months. This way you always know that your foods are providing you with the best nutrition and taste possible. Always eat the food with the closest date. Check www.waltonfeed.com/grain.faqs/default.htm or www.idir.net/~medintz/surv_faq/asciifaq.txt for more code deciphering.

Gardening

You may want to give some consideration to putting in a good garden as soon as the weather allows. Many of our fresh fruits and vegetables come from South and Central American countries. You may want to buy and store all needed tools, fertilizers, seeds, insecticides (go organic), etc. When buying seeds, get non-hybrid seeds. Non-hybrid seeds regenerate—the seeds created from their plants can be stored and reused the next year. Hybrid seeds, a genetically altered seed developed and heavily promoted by seed companies to make more money, will only grow once. The seeds from their plants are sterile. Fresh seeds will last 5–10 years if kept cool and dry.[1]

Freeze-dried or Dehydrated Foods

Another way to store your needed foods is to order what is called "preparedness," "reserve," or "emergency" food from a company specializing in these products.[2] These foods, which are either freeze-dried or dehydrated, offer several benefits in food storage (Figure 2.5). These advantages are:

- They are lightweight (as they contain little water).
- They are compact.
- They are more nutritious than many canned foods.
- Their shelf life is often 10 to 20 years.
- They can be bought as a complete system, in prepacks of one week to one year.
- They are delivered to your home packaged and ready to store.

Figure 2.5   Freeze-dried and dehydrated (low-moisture) foods are often packed in #10 cans (approximately one gallon). You can store more food in less space with these products.

- Most reputable companies are careful to supply all the needed calories and nutrients.

Perhaps the biggest drawback to this option, other than the cost of the more expensive freeze-dried packages, is that if you do not need these foods, if your normal food supply is not interrupted or is quickly restored, then you may not want to eat these foods that are not as tasty as what you are used to.

The purchase of a system represents an investment of between $300 (for basic dehydrated) to $2500 (for better tasting freeze-dried) per person per year. Also, some products are "taste challenged," so be sure you test a few samples before ordering.

Dehydrated and freeze-dried packaging involves storing dehydrated, dried, and freeze-dried foods in pre-packed cans, cartons, etc. Compared to typical consumer food prices in the supermarket, many dehydrated food storage items may be less per serving than the grocery store. Buyers making selective choices normally find great value in dehydrated, dried, and freeze-dried foods in pre-packed cans or bulk foods. Virtually every food storage supplier has the capability of selling a prepackaged plan or "program" of selected fruits, grains, meats or simulated meats, and vegetables in #10 cans or in bulk. These "programs" can be "one person/one year" or "family of four/six months," etc. These suppliers also provide individual food items from open stock.

Be sure to deal with a reputable company. This is not a large industry. Costs and claims of "feeds family of four for a year" can be confusing. You can buy a one-person, one-year package for as little as $298, but it is almost all rice, grains, beans, and other staples. True, you won't starve that year, but you won't look forward to any meal that year either. You really need to analyze each food package to see how much is basic staples and how much is the better tasting freeze-dried or dehydrated products. This can be rather complex to do.

SELECTING A FOOD RESERVE SYSTEM

Some day you may actually need to depend on a food reserve system. The purchase of a system represents a sizable investment. The consumer should be discriminating in selecting the manufacturer. The questions and information below provide a valuable process by which one can identify and determine the most suitable food reserve system.

The following questions will assist you in identifying a system for you and your family:

1. Under what scenarios do you anticipate the need for using food reserves?
2. Will you be mobile?
3. Will food preparation facilities, supplies, and fuel be available?
4. Have you determined the length of time you desire the system to sustain you and your family?
5. How many people will be depending upon your food?
6. Are there special nutritional requirements?

7. How important is ease of preparation?
8. Have you considered your budget?
9. How many calories do you require per person?

Considerations:

1. PURITY OF INGREDIENTS—Are foods all natural with no artificial preservatives, flavorings, colorings, MSG, or white sugar?
2. FAMILIARITY—Your food system should be familiar everyday foods easily recognizable and reflect a balanced diet offering good taste.
3. PREPARATION CONVENIENCE—Can food systems be prepared with a limited amount of fuel and water?
4. SHELF LIFE—Shelf life of any food reserves is always critical. Excessive heat will shorten the shelf life of all products. A rule of thumb: the cooler the better.
5. PROPER ROTATION—It is important to rotate food reserves into your daily diet.

Packaging

Most freeze-dried and dehydrated products are packed in #10 size cans (approximately one gallon) or #2½ size cans (approximately one quart). These cans are heavy-gauge metal and enamel coated both inside and out. Nitrogen flush (inert gas) and the use of a "state of the art" oxygen absorber in #10 size cans are often used to eliminate oxygen. Both procedures insure the very best in shelf life. Resealable plastic lids are often included in the systems.

Freeze-dried Foods[2]

For instant or quick rehydration of certain dried foods and for products which retain their shape and texture, freeze-drying is the preferred method (Figure 2.6). The first step in freeze-drying is to rapidly freeze the food. The water content, now frozen, is turned directly into a gas and withdrawn from the food during the next steps, vacuum and

Figure 2.6 Freeze-dried foods can last 10–20 years. They look and taste like the real thing but can be a little costly. Note smaller one-meal packages.

heat, thus avoiding the shrinkage. Freeze-dried products include grains, beans, fruits, meats, seafood, pastas, vegetables, and eggs. Often these ingredients are packaged as a complete meal, such as beef Strogonoff or chicken Alfredo, and you just add boiling water.

Freeze-dried foods, the most expensive of the preparedness foods, are also the most flavorful. Many of the meals are quite enjoyable and remain very close to their original taste, smell, and texture. You can keep them stored for 10–20 years, or eat them as part of your standard diet.

Advantages of freeze-dried products:

- They retain the original taste and nutritional value of the food.
- Foods are quick and easy to prepare.
- There is no waste.
- It is an ideal method for maintaining flavors of meat, poultry, and fish.
- Extends the shelf life of the product.
- No preservatives are necessary.
- Results in a super-lightweight/compact product.

- A wide variety of foods are available.
- Can be packaged as complete meals—not just individual dishes.

Disadvantages of freeze-dried products:

- Can be expensive.
- Some may be "taste challenged."

Dehydrated Foods

The standard method of dehydrating vegetables and spices is to place the items on a conveyor belt and run them through an oven at a high temperature for a relatively short time (Figure 2.7). Between 90% and 95% of the moisture is removed. Drying is the oldest known form of food preservation. For example, the Egyptians sun dried various foods for the Pharaohs; a roasted meal called Pulmenturh was the principal field ration of the Roman legions; and, our American Indians had their pemmican and jerkies. While the technical reasons may have escaped

Figure 2.7   Dehydrated foods will store for 10–20 years and are relatively inexpensive. Be sure you try some samples as some of the products are excellent, while others "taste-challenged."

those earlier generations, they all discovered that dried foods kept better and were the only way they could keep variety and quality in their diets.

In the raw state, fruits, vegetables, and most other foods contain 80% to 90% water. That water, in combination with heat and/or oxygen, is the principal cause of food spoilage. Hence, the elimination of most of the original moisture from foods extends their shelf life and natural goodness. Since minerals are stable during heat, oxidation, and storage, the major changes in the nutritional stability and values of foods occur in vitamins. Acidity, alkalinity, heat, light, percent of oxygen, storage temperature, and time are the principal factors that affect the stability of vitamins. Low-moisture foods that are packed in sealed containers from which most of the residual oxygen has been removed and replaced with nitrogen usually retain or sustain higher levels of vitamin stability than is possible with other forms of food. That stability is further protected when such low-moisture foods are stored at constant temperatures of 72°F, or lower.

Some vegetables are more suited to this form of drying than others. This means that with the addition of water, the product rehydrates back to its original state more easily. Preferable items include onions, bell peppers, tomatoes, celery, carrots, and mushrooms. Dehydrated items such as peas, corn, and green beans do not rehydrate as well as freeze-dried. Dehydrated meats are not available so many dehydrated food companies use a vegetable substitute that is flavored to resemble various meats.

You can dehydrate many of your own foods with an air or electric dehydrator (Figure 2.8). However, sometimes this can be more costly than purchasing the food already dried.

Low-moisture (dehydrated) foods that are purchased in quantity and used frequently as components in everyday meals are as economical and often times more so than other forms of food when the following factors are considered:

- No seasonal price or quality variances.
- Requires no refrigeration or freezing.
- No leftovers or waste.
- No spoilage.
- No peeling, coring, trimming, or washing.

Figure 2.8   This electric unit lets you dehydrate many of your own foods. However, electric units may be worthless if the power goes out.

Advantages of dehydrated products:

- Foods are quick and easy to prepare.
- No preservatives are necessary.
- Results in a super-lightweight/compact product.
  - Long shelf life
  - Cost-efficient food option
- Provide year-round fresh appearance and taste.
- Require no refrigeration, freezing, or other expensive, energy-dependent storage.
- Require much less space than other forms of food.
- Are not subject to infestation or bacteria growth.

- Are easily and quickly measured into precise servings that eliminate leftovers and waste.
- Are ideal for most kinds of special diets.

Disadvantages of dehydrated products:

- Some may be "taste-challenged."
- A limited variety of foods are available.
- Can be slow to reconstitute.

A Good-tasting Meat Replacement

Meat can be a problem in food storage. Freeze dried meat is expensive and can be "taste challenged." However, there is a good tasting alternative. The leader in offering cost effective dehydrated meat replacement products is a company called Global Village Market (Figure 2.9).

Global Village Market offers "The Greatest" beef, burger, and chicken. These are soy meat substitutes that have been labeled by the prestigious Pasteur Institute as "the food of the future." These products are made from the filet of the soybean known as the soy-isolate, which is very nutritious, providing the perfect protein source with complete amino acids. These meat alternatives have no saturated fat or cholesterol, and are high in fiber. Because these products are dehydrated, they require no refrigeration or freezing and have an extended shelf life, making them perfect for food storage or preparedness.

Figure 2.9 Global Village Market makes an excellent meat substitute product that is tasty, healthy, and inexpensive.

In addition to these meat alternatives, the company also offers soy snack and meal replacement bars, lactose-free shakes, and Icelandic "miracle salt."

Global Village Market's objective is to help end world hunger. To achieve this objective the company has a philanthropic arm known as the Global Village Champions, which is supported by high profile individuals such as Muhammad Ali, Celine Dion, Gary U.S. Bonds, Michael Johnson, and Guy Lafleur. To date, the company has donated in excess of 50 million meals.

PROPER FOOD STORAGE

The preferred method of storing foods is to store everything inside in your living space. This keeps them dry, away from extreme heat and cold (not above 70° and not below freezing), and hopefully rodents. You can make use of normal pantries and closets and then consider other storage areas. There is a lot of room under beds, under furniture, on top of kitchen cabinets, in a corner, in a guest room, etc.

If storing inside is impossible, garages and sheds can be considered, but extreme heat, cold, moisture, and rodents may make some foods unusable—a harsh reality if you ever need them. Canned goods should do okay in an unheated garage if temperatures can be moderated, even if it means a small heater on bitter cold nights (Figures 2.10, 2.11). Always leave your canned goods in cardboard boxes, if they came in them. It helps insulate the food. If your area is very cold, you may want to buy the Styrofoam that comes in sheets like plywood and wrap it around your stored food to help prevent freezing. A deep freeze that lasts several days may burst a canned product in an unheated garage. However, if the canned goods freeze even a little, their nutritional value is diminished.

Figure 2.10   If you must keep your food in the garage, protect it from freezing, extreme heat, and rodents.

Figure 2.11   Each storage shed can hold more than a year's supply of preparedness food for two people. Water in background is two-month supply for two people.

Your canned and jarred products can store easily for as long as the "sell by" or "use by" date listed on each. Even after this date, they can be consumed safely for quite awhile. The "sell by" date has a large margin of error in these types of food. Foods that are packaged in plastic or paper bags or boxes should be stored unopened in plastic buckets or boxes to further protect them from moisture and rodents (Figure 2.12). You may want to place a moisture or oxygen absorber in each bucket. Keep food covered at all times.

Basically, there are four factors that affect food storage to keep in mind:

- Temperature
- Light
- Humidity
- Vermin infestation

Figure 2.12 Bulk foods can be stored in plastic buckets like these. Also leave all foods in their original packaging. The lid in front is a "screw-on" type, which makes opening much easier.

STORAGE TIPS

- Foods should be kept dry and cool, in a dark area, if possible (not above 70° and not below freezing).
- Keep food covered at all times.
- Exercise the First In-First Out (FIFO) principle.
- Do not place food directly on cold floors or against exterior walls.
- Open food containers carefully so that you can close them tightly after each use.
- Crackers, cereals, cookies, and breads should be kept in plastic bags, then in tight containers.
- Store packages of sugar, dried fruits, and nuts in screw-top jars or airtight cans to protect them from pests.
- Put other boxed foods like cereals in tightly closed cans or metal containers.
- Inspect all food containers for signs of spoilage before using.
- Rotate foods as you can, dating your food supply. Inspect your food periodically.

Refrigeration

Needless to say, if the power goes out, so will your freezer and refrigerator. However, there are some things you can do to keep your foods cold. Food can stay usable in both the freezer and the refrigerator for several days, if the doors are not opened too often. If the power goes out, wrap blankets around the freezer or refrigerator. This will help insulate them and keep the food even longer.

It would be a good idea to have several large picnic-type coolers (Figure 2.13). You can place food in these and set them outside in colder areas and this will keep food cold. Also there are refrigerators available that run on propane (LP) gas. These are available through your propane dealer. If you have one of these and a 500 to 1000 gallon above-ground or buried tank, you're set for refrigeration without electricity.

Figure 2.13   The cooler on the right will work better than the refrigerator if the power goes out. You can buy propane refrigerators which do not need electricity.

HOUSEHOLD SUNDRIES

It takes more than food to supply yourself with everything you need to make meal preparation run as smoothly as possible. For example, make sure you have a nonelectric can opener, a grain grinder, and disposable utensils (Figure 2.14).

Here are some other items to include on your shopping preparedness list:

- Paper plates, napkins, cups to reduce the need for washing dishes
- Aluminum foil (better than dirtying pans)
- Heavy-duty Zip lock bags of all sizes

Figure 2.14   A good grain grinder would be a good item to add to your food collection.

- Mcasuring cups/spoons
- Trash bags
- Disposable baby bottle liners, if needed
- Several nonelectric can openers

NOTES

[1] Seeds Blum Co., (800) 528-3658, www.sseedsblum.com
[2] We recommend the companies listed at the end of the chapter as they have been in the industry for many years and have a known product.
[3] Global Village, (514) 396-3385, Mention #5061

RECOMMENDED FREEZE-DRIED FOOD COMPANIES

- FOOD PLUS (distributors for AlpineAire), 1-877-FOOD-PLUS, www.foodplusonline.com
- NITRO-PAK, 1-800-866-4876, www.nitro-pak.com

RECOMMENDED DEHYDRATED FOOD COMPANIES

- GLOBAL VILLAGE 514 396-3385, extension #5061
- NITRO-PAK, 1-800-866-4876, www.nitro-pak.com
- MILLENNIUM III FOODS, 1-888-883-1603, www.millennium3foods.com

KITCHEN CHECKLIST

(Courtesy of Y2K Women, www.y2kwomen.com)

Pantry

VARIETY OF BEANS

- ❑ Great Northern
- ❑ Kidney beans
- ❑ Lentils
- ❑ Navy
- ❑ Pinto
- ❑ Red beans
- ❑ Sprouting peas, etc.
- ❑ _____
- ❑ _____

RICE AND GRAINS

- ❑ Barley
- ❑ Cold cereals

❑ Corn (popcorn and field corn)
❑ Flour (wheat, white, and other varieties)
❑ Instant hot cereals (oatmeal, Cream of Wheat, etc.)
❑ Rice (brown, white, or combination)
❑ _____
❑ _____

MEAT AND FISH

❑ Chicken
❑ Corned beef
❑ Salmon
❑ Soy protein—Taco filling, BBQ Beef, etc.
❑ Spam
❑ Tuna
❑ _____
❑ _____

COOKING AGENTS

❑ Baking powder
❑ Baking soda
❑ Butter-flavored Crisco
❑ Shortening (like Crisco)
❑ Olive oil (stores best)
❑ Vegetable oil (canola stores well)
❑ Mayonnaise (small jars if there is no refrigeration)
❑ Yeast (in a pinch you can use sourdough)
❑ _____
❑ _____

SALT

❑ Iodized
❑ Rock salt
❑ Sea salt
❑ _____
❑ _____

SWEETENERS

- ❏ White sugar
- ❏ Brown sugar
- ❏ Corn syrup
- ❏ Equal or Sweet n' Low (just to have on hand for us diehards!)
- ❏ Honey
- ❏ Maple syrup
- ❏ Molasses
- ❏ Powdered sugar
- ❏ _____

PASTA

- ❏ Macaroni
- ❏ Shells
- ❏ Spaghetti (with jars of heat-up sauce)
- ❏ _____
- ❏ _____

DAIRY PRODUCTS

- ❏ Dry Buttermilk
- ❏ Milk (canned evaporated)
- ❏ Parmesan cheese
- ❏ Powdered butter/margarine (like Butter Busters)
- ❏ Powdered eggs
- ❏ Cheese powder (This sounded gross to me until I realized it was what was in the boxes of prepared macaroni and cheese!)
- ❏ _____
- ❏ _____

VEGETABLES: CANNED, DEHYDRATED, OR FREEZE-DRIED

- ❏ Dehydrated beets
- ❏ Dehydrated broccoli
- ❏ Dehydrated cabbage
- ❏ Canned and bottled vegetables
- ❏ Carrots
- ❏ Celery

- ❑ Creamed corn
- ❑ Green beans
- ❑ Instant mashed potatoes
- ❑ Peas
- ❑ Soup and stew blends
- ❑ Spinach

FRUITS: CANNED, DEHYDRATED, OR FREEZE-DRIED

- ❑ Apples
- ❑ Applesauce
- ❑ Apricots
- ❑ Bananas
- ❑ Canned and bottled fruit juices
- ❑ Flavored apples
- ❑ Canned fruit cocktail
- ❑ Lemon juice (bottled does not have to be refrigerated)
- ❑ Oranges
- ❑ Canned peaches
- ❑ Raisins
- ❑ Variety of dehydrated fruits
- ❑ _____

SOUPS

- ❑ Canned chicken/beef stock
- ❑ Soup starter
- ❑ Variety of canned soups (chicken noodle, vegetable, tomato, cream of mushroom, broccoli, etc.)
- ❑ Instant soups (like Ramen or any soup you just add water to)
- ❑ _____
- ❑ _____

SPICES AND FLAVORINGS

- ❑ Baking cocoa
- ❑ Basil
- ❑ Bouillon (beef and chicken)
- ❑ Canned tomatoes

- ❏ Chili powder
- ❏ Cinnamon
- ❏ Garlic (powder, minced, salt)
- ❏ Green peppers
- ❏ Ketchup (Tomato products are a regular in most American kids' diets and they will often eat things with ketchup on them they wouldn't otherwise. Ketchup is high in sugar and kids are almost addicted to it!)
- ❏ Mustard
- ❏ Onions (powder, flakes, salt)
- ❏ Oregano
- ❏ Pepper
- ❏ Salad dressing
- ❏ Salsa
- ❏ Soy sauce
- ❏ Teriyaki sauce
- ❏ Tomato paste
- ❏ Tomato powder
- ❏ Tomato sauce
- ❏ Vinegar (plain and flavored)
- ❏ Worchestershire sauce
- ❏ Bay leaves (I've found bay leaves are great for keeping bugs out of flour and cereal so you might want to get an extra large bottle!)

SEEDS FOR SPROUTING: (ESSENTIAL FOR VITAMINS)

- ❏ Alfalfa
- ❏ Mung
- ❏ Radish
- ❏ Sprouting peas
- ❏ Lentils

FRESH ROOT VEGETABLES

- ❏ Butternut squash
- ❏ Potatoes (kept in cool, dark place)
- ❏ Waxed rutabagas
- ❏ _____
- ❏ _____

ODDS AND ENDS

- ❑ Biscuit mix
- ❑ Canned mushrooms
- ❑ Cans of nuts (peanuts, cashews, etc.)
- ❑ Cereals
- ❑ Crackers
- ❑ Pancake mix
- ❑ Pickles
- ❑ Salad dressing mix (Italian, Ranch—Good Seasons type)
- ❑ Waffle mix
- ❑ _____
- ❑ _____

BEVERAGES

- ❑ Coffee (vacuum sealed but already ground if there is a problem with electricity)
- ❑ Gatorade
- ❑ Hot chocolate
- ❑ Individual coffee bags
- ❑ Instant coffee
- ❑ Noncarbonated drink mix (like Tang, Kool-aid, etc.)
- ❑ Non dairy creamer
- ❑ Sodas (I have lots of friends who say they won't survive without Diet Coke!)
- ❑ Small boxes of juice for kids
- ❑ Tea
- ❑ Wine in boxes with Mylar bags
- ❑ _____
- ❑ _____

QUICK AND EASY TO PREPARE FOODS

- ❑ Canned chili, canned soups, canned meats, peanut butter, etc.
- ❑ Freeze-dried or dried or no-cook foods
- ❑ Macaroni and cheese
- ❑ Spaghetti sauce
- ❑ _____

PSYCHOLOGICAL FOODS OR COMFORT FOODS

❏ Brownie mixes
❏ Cake mixes
❏ Cheerios
❏ Chocolate chips
❏ Chocolate milk mix
❏ Dream Whip mix
❏ Hard candies
❏ JELL-O
❏ Jelly
❏ Popcorn
❏ Puddings
❏ _____
❏ _____

BABY FOOD AND FORMULA

(Note: I absolutely encourage breast feeding! However, if a woman is under stress from a crisis, it is very possible for her not to have an adequate milk supply. Supplementation may be necessary!)

❏ Powdered formula (A pediatrician I spoke with said canned formula wouldn't last as long and was more expensive. Have some bottles of sterile water on hand to mix with the formula.)
❏ Pureed fruits and vegetables
❏ Hand grinder to puree table food
❏ _____
❏ _____

VITAMINS

❏ Children's liquid or chewable vitamins
❏ Liquid dietary supplement (like Ensure)
❏ Mineral supplements (like calcium)
❏ Multivitamins
❏ Vitamin C

WATER

- ❑ Drinking water
- ❑ Distilled water
- ❑ Soda water
- ❑ Water for cleaning and bathing

Cupboards
COOKING UTENSILS

- ❑ French press coffeepot (the kind you add hot water to, let steep, and then press the grounds down)
- ❑ Pressure cooker
- ❑ Kettle
- ❑ Cast iron cookware
- ❑ Skillet
- ❑ Dutch oven
- ❑ Bread pans
- ❑ Waffle iron
- ❑ Griddle
- ❑ Wok
- ❑ Plastic storage containers
- ❑ _____

CHECKLIST GARAGE

- ❑ Dog/cat food in airtight containers (like metal garbage cans) to keep rodents out
- ❑ Kitty litter
- ❑ Pet supplies (vitamins, pet medications like heartworm preventative, flea and tick treatments, chew toys, shampoo, etc.)
- ❑ Bug extermination
- ❑ Ant, roach, spider killer
- ❑ Bee/wasp killer
- ❑ Rat/mouse traps
- ❑ Fly traps
- ❑ _____
- ❑ _____

FOOD SHELF-LIFE RECOMMENDATIONS
From "How-To Survival Library"
(http://www.y2klibrary.com)

Food Product	Storage Life in Months
STAPLES	
Baking powder	18 or exp. date
Baking soda	24
Bisquick	Exp. date
Bouillon	24
Cereals	6–12
Chocolate	12
Pre-melted	18
Semi-sweet	18
Chocolate syrup	24
Coffee	24
Coffee lighteners (dry)	9
Cornmeal	12
Cornstarch	18
Country Time lemonade drink mix	24
Crystal Lite drink mix	24
Tang drink mix	24
Kool-Aid drink mix	18–24
White flour	6–8
Whole wheat	6–8
Gelatin, all types	18
Jell-O	24
Grits	12
Honey	12
Jellies, jams	12
Marshmallow cream	3–4
Mayonnaise	2–3
Milk: condensed	12
Milk: evaporated	12
Molasses	12+

Pasta	24
White rice	24+
Minute rice	18
Bottled salad dressings	10–12
Salad oils	6
Oil—Crisco or Puritan	24
Corn oil	18
Crisco Shortening	Indef.
Vinegar	Indef.
Salt	Indef.
Sugar	Indef.
Sugar: brown	18
Sugar: confectioners	24+
Sugar: granulated	24+
Syrups	12
Tea	18
Tea bags	36
Tea: instant	24

MIXES AND PACKAGED FOODS

Biscuit, brownie, Muffin mix	9
Cake mixes	9
Casseroles, complete or add own meat	9–12
Cookies	2–3 wks
Krusteaz mixes	24
Pillsbury mixes	18
Betty Crocker mixes	8–12+
Jiffy mixes	24
Crackers	3
Stove Top Stuffing Mix	Exp. Date
Frosting mix	3
Frostings: canned	8
Hot roll mix	18
Pancake mix	6–9
Pie crust mix	8
Pies and pastries	2–3 days

Potatoes; instant	6–12
Pudding mixes	12
Rice mixes	6
Rice-a-Roni	Exp. Date
Pasta-Roni	Exp. Date
Rice & Sauce	10–15
Noodles & Sauce	12–24
Pasta & Sauce	9–12
Sauce/gravy mix	6–12
Soup mix	12
Soup base	120
Country Kitchen soup	36
Toaster pastries	2–3

CANNED AND DRIED FOODS

Canned baby foods	12
Canned tomato sauce	12
Canned cheese sauce	24–36
Canned tuna, fish & seafood	5 years
Canned cranberry sauce	Exp. Date
Canned fruits	36+
Canned fruit pie fillings	24–36
Dinty Moore	Indef.
Spam	Indef.
Ham chunks	Indef.
Chili	Indef.
Dried beef	Indef.
Black Label ham	Exp. Date
Canned meat	36
Canned chicken	36
Canned soup	Exp. Date
Canned tomatoes	36+
Canned vegetables	24–48
Canned baked beans	24–36
Canned black beans	24
Canned French fried onions	24

Ragu spaghetti sauce	Exp. Date
Five Brothers pasta sauce	24
Canned fruit juices	6
Juices, bottled	12–24
Dried fruits	6
Dried vegetables	12
Dried peas & beans	12

SPICES, HERBS, CONDIMENTS, AND EXTRACTS

Ketchup	18–24
Chili sauce	24
Mustard, yellow prepared	24
Jar pickles	12–24
Spices	12–24
Steak sauce	24
Tabasco sauce	60
Extracts	24
Vanilla	12
Vegetables, dehydrated flakes	6

OTHER

Cheese, Parmesan grated	10
Coconut, shredded canned or pkg.	12
Meat substitutes TVP (Textured Vegetable Protein)	12
Imitation bacon bits	12
Nut	4
Nuts (In shell) pkg.	24
Nutmeats pkg.	3
Peanut butter	6–9
Jif Peanut Butter	24
Popcorn	24
Freeze-dried mushrooms	24
Whipped topping (dry)	12
Yeast (dry)	Exp. date

STORING AND TREATING WATER

"When microprocessors at Coff's Harbor water storage facility were turned in to 2000 dates in a simulation, the entire chemical holdings—normally used in carefully regulated amounts to purify water—were dumped into the water in one hit. Experts say this would have the potential to kill the town's entire population."
—From the *Sun Herald,* an Australian newspaper, April 26, 1998

THE PROBLEM

Nothing is more essential than water. Without it we would die in several days (as compared to weeks without food). Without it disease is born and spread, cleanliness becomes impossible, modern life degenerates quickly. Unless a disaster is so catastrophic as to cripple all governmental services, any interruption of our water supply will be quickly restored (obviously this may not be the case if you use your own well. See "Wells" at the end of this chapter). However, the water delivery may be only for several hours per day and the water may not be safe. And there is always the possibility of no water at all for awhile.

Therefore, you must have clean, drinkable water stored and available to you before any event.

Local water companies may draw on a water source hundreds of miles away. This requires computers and pumps and valves, which are needed to keep the water flowing. Water treatment, such as the addition of chlorine, is controlled by computers. Another problem that may occur if we lose heat and/or water in the middle of winter is that the pipes can freeze and burst. When the water is restored and the pipes thaw, your house may be flooded. Be sure to turn off the water into your home and to drain the existing water in your system by opening the lowest faucets if your pipes are in danger of freezing. Also be careful in using the water immediately after water service is restored. The first supply coming through the system may be silty or contaminated. Don't use it as drinking water until local officials have declared it safe.

Using contaminated water for drinking or cooking can lead to problems which range from a minor upset stomach, such as you'd have with the flu, to life-threatening illnesses, such as amoebic dysentery, viral infection, cholera, typhoid, or hepatitis. Also, disasters may lead to environmental pollution. Chemicals may get into our water supplies from storage yards, manufacturing plants, etc., that experience a computer failure. A chemical leak in Bhopal, India several years ago killed 1,200 people and devastated a community. In fact, if you live near a potentially dangerous environmental threat (chemical, nuclear plant, etc.) be sure you know the best escape routes should a disaster occur. Because of all this, you must have a stored supply of clean water and a way to treat more water until normal water delivery is restored.

THE SOLUTIONS

Water Storage

As with food, in the event of a possible disruption of our infrastructure (power, water, transportation, etc.), we recommend a minimum of 2–4 weeks' supply of clean, drinkable water, for each family member, be stored. However, should you feel that more storage, say for 6 to 12 months, is best, there are water storage products on the market for large-volume storage of water. Be sure to store water that you are used to drinking, water from your own tap. This will avoid any problems created by adjusting to new water. Before the event this is rather an easy and inexpensive task to do. After the event, who knows.

If your supplies begin to run low, remember: Never ration water. Drink the amount you need today, and try to find more for tomorrow. You can minimize the amount of water your body needs by reducing activity and staying cool.

Drinkable water should be stored in new, thoroughly cleaned, heavy-duty, plastic containers with tight-fitting lids. Be sure your containers are food grade and approved for water storage by the FDA. If you are also storing water for bathing and clothes washing, this can be stored in any uncontaminated container (new large garbage cans will work and are very cheap). Clean glass containers can also be used, but breakage (especially if the water freezes) and weight are a problem with these. Avoid metal containers as they can rust (except stainless steel). Never use a container that has held toxic substances, because tiny amounts may remain in the container's pores.

For drinking water, avoid reusing light-weight food grade containers, such as used milk and drink containers. Milk containers will leave a taste. These containers can also freeze and burst. However, cleaned two-liter drink containers can be used if freezing is not a factor and the budget is (see Figure 3.1). Also be sure water is stored away from paint, chemicals, fertilizers, and petroleum products; the objectionable odors can penetrate the "breathable" bottles. Water should not be stored where it will get over 100 degrees, freeze, or be in direct sunlight. Before using any containers, even new ones, wash them out with baking soda and warm water and rinse with clean water.

Store the water you are presently drinking so no adjustment will be necessary. You will need one gallon per person per day for drinking and cooking (more for children, nursing mothers, people with illnesses, in hot areas, or when doing physical exercise). For staying clean, extra water is needed. Another gallon per day per person is recommended for cleaning (and yet more if you plan to flush toilets). Remember pets will also need water. If you are a family of four, stor-

Figure 3.1 If necessary, water can be stored in clean two-liter drink bottles. However, these can freeze and burst. Heavy duty water containers are preferred.

ing water for two weeks, you will need to store 4 people × 1 gal/day × 15 days = 60 gallons of water. Another 60 gallons is recommended for improved cleaning. That's 120 gallons. This can be accomplished with 120 one-gallon containers, 25 five-gallon, 4 thirty-gallon or one 125-gallon (Figure 3.2). As with food, rotate the water on an ongoing basis so that it keeps its quality and taste.

The choice of what size containers to use depends on several factors. Space wise, a large 250-gallon may not work. If a tank this large is stored on a deck or second floor, be sure it can hold the weight. These large tanks are cumbersome to use, but most have spigots so you can easily draw off smaller amounts. Large water tanks can be placed outside or in the garage (if it does not freeze), inside the house, or in the attic but only directly over a load-bearing wall. You can get these in rigid tanks for $200–500 or in inflatable bladders for about $100.00 (Figure 3.3). 200-gallon FDA-approved inflatable blad-

Figure 3.2 Water containers come in everything from 5 to 50,000 gallons. These 5- and 55-gallon containers work well for residential use.

Figure 3.3 These 200-gallon water bags cost only $90. They store enough water for 4 people for 50 days.

ders are available for about $100.00. You can even get larger bladders that hold 700–2,000 gallons.[1] Waterbeds can be used (around 350 gallons), but use these only for washing and bathing, not drinking, unless it is a new waterbed without algacide in the water.

Mid-size water tanks, 30–100 gallons, are also very affordable. You can get a FDA-approved 55-gallon drum for $38.00 (Figure 3.4). Plastic companies make 5–6 gallon water cans for around $8–$10 (Figure 3.5).

Figure 3.4   Fifty-five-gallon water drums cost under $40. Note hand pump for transferring water to smaller containers. Also note metal lid opener.

Figure 3.5   Five-gallon containers work well and are often stackable.

Try to find one that is stackable so you can save space. If you are using the larger tanks, be sure you buy either a hand pump or a battery-operated pump to transfer the water to smaller containers (Figure 3.6).

The 5- or 35-gallon plastic drums are not particularly portable. There are flexible 5-gallon plastic water containers that have the advantage of folding up completely when empty and some flexibility when full (Figure 3.7). If you need to travel, these are a good idea. There are also portable 5-gallon showers available in most camping sections of department stores.

In many areas, where rainfall is scarce, people use cisterns. A cistern is usually a tank built into the ground that catches and stores rainwater that has been diverted from rooftops, porches, etc. (a 2"-rain can collect 150–300 gallons). By building it into the ground, it keeps the water cool, which in turn prohibits the growth of bacteria. Though earlier models were built from brick or mortar, you can now use plastic or metal containers.

Figure 3.6   Small water pumps can be hooked to a car battery and used to transfer water from large containers to small ones.

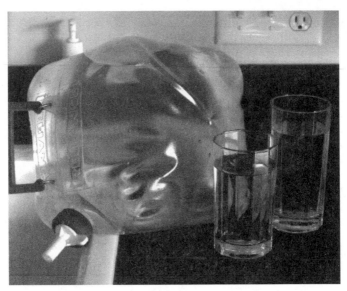

Figure 3.7   These collapsible water jugs hold 2.5 gallons and are easily stored when empty.

Since most houses are already equipped with a gutters, a cistern system can actually be quite easy to set up. You can just divert your gutters into 55-gallon drinking water drums, tanks, waterbeds, or even into a large plastic swimming pool. Many people choose to divert the first few minutes of the rainwater away from the cistern; this washes away dirt, debris, pollutants, bugs, etc. Put some fine screen over the ends of the gutters or hoses to filter out large particles, and then treat the water for drinking as outlined below. Also cover it from sunlight, which promotes growth of algae.

As you store your water, you may want to add aerobic oxygen to it. This has stabilized oxygen molecules that kill anaerobic (infectious) bacteria while leaving untouched bacteria that are harmless or good for you. It also aerates the water by adding oxygen to it, which keeps some harmful bacteria from growing in it. The added oxygen is also considered a health benefit when the water is consumed. You can store water for up to 10 years with aerobic oxygen added to it, but it is a little costly at about $14.00 to treat 50–75 gallons (Figure 3.8).

Figure 3.8 You can add stabilized oxygen to your water to help kill bacteria. A good option but a little costly.

Normal Water Usage Drinking and Cooking

Shower (1 per day):	25 gallons
Toilet flush (10 flushes @ 3 gallons each):	30 gallons
Hand washing (Twice @ 2 gallons each time):	4 gallons
Brushing teeth (Twice @ 1/2 gallon each time):	1 gallon
Drinking and cooking:	2 gallons
Total:	63 gallons

Low Water Usage Drinking and Cooking

Shower (1 solar shower or sponge bath every other day):	2 gallons (optional)
Toilet flush (with use of boat potty, composting toilet, etc.):	1 gallon
Hand washing (Twice @ 1/4 gallons each time):	½ gallon
Brushing teeth (Twice @ 1/8 gallon each time):	¼ gallon
Drinking and cooking:	1 gallons
Total:	4¾ gallons

LOCATING AND TREATING WATER

If a disaster catches you without a stored supply of clean water, you can use water in your hot-water tank, in your plumbing, and in ice cubes. As a last resort, you can use water in the reservoir tank of your toilet (not the bowl), but purify it first.

Water beds hold up to 400 gallons, but some water beds contain toxic chemicals that may not be fully removed by many purifiers. If you designate a water bed in your home as an emergency resource, drain it yearly and refill it with fresh water containing two ounces of bleach per 120 gallons. You may use the water for toilet flushing only.

To use the water in your pipes, let air into the plumbing by turning on the highest (elevation) faucet in your house and draining the water from the lowest one. To use the water in your hot-water tank, be sure the electricity or gas is off, and open the drain at the bottom of the tank. Start the water flowing by turning off the water intake valve and turning on a hot-water faucet. Do not turn on the gas or electricity when the tank is empty.

Do you know the location of your incoming water valve? You'll need to shut if off to stop contaminated water from entering your home if you hear reports of broken water or sewage lines. Also, in cold climates, frozen pipes may burst if there is no heat. Shut off the water and drain the pipes if there's a strong possibility of this occurring.

If you need to find water outside your home, be sure to purify the water before drinking it. Avoid water with floating material, an odor, or dark color. Use salt water only if you distill it first. You should not drink flood water. Outdoor water sources include rainwater, streams and rivers, ponds and lakes, natural springs, and snow.

Locating additional water may be as obvious as looking around the house. Before a possible disaster you may want to fill all sinks, bathtubs, hot tubs, pools (even inflatable pools can hold a lot of water). Your hot water heater can hold 30–50 gallons. Local creeks, ponds, lakes, springs, etc., are also sources of water, though obviously this water must be treated before it is consumed (Figure 3.9).

Never drink questionable water unless it has been properly treated. Contaminated water can threaten your health, even your life. Bad water can cause anything from stomach problems to such life-threat-

Figure 3.9   Water from most lakes, creeks, and springs can all be used for drinking if properly treated.

ening illnesses as amoebic dysentery, cholera, typhoid, hepatitis, or viral infection.

To treat any questionable water you can either boil it, chemically treat it, or run it through a water purifier. Remember, just because water is clear does not mean it is safe. You can get water from any stream, creek, or lake, and if properly treated, it will be perfectly safe. Be sure you have identified possible sources of water before the event. Before purifying, let any suspended particles settle to the bottom, or strain them through layers of paper towel or clean cloth.

No matter which option you choose to go with, be sure you understand how to properly treat water. Your health or life may depend on it. Getting sick in a disaster may be problematic if medical facilities are strained. There are several approaches to treating water:

- Water purifiers and filters
- Chemical treatment
- Boiling

Water Purifiers and Filters

A quality water purifier or filter is highly recommended. However, the water filters that can be purchased at many retail stores are not as effective as quality water purifiers and filters, and most are not suited for emergency preparedness. The standards that filters sold in many retail stores must meet are much lower than those for purifiers. Some good water purifiers (General Ecology, Katadyn, Epic Water, British Berkefeld, Pur, Sweet Water, etc.)[2] can remove not only chemical contaminants like pesticides, insecticides, PCBs, etc., but many can also remove pathogens and bacteria, such as Giardia and Cryptosporidia. Cryptosporidia, or Crypto, is the most frequent cause of water-borne illness in the United States today. In 1993, it caused 400,000 illnesses and more than 100 deaths in Milwaukee. Though Crypto can be

Figure 3.10   Portable hand-pumped water purifiers like these effectively treat any water by passing it through a filter. This model removes all harmful contaminants and bacteria.

Figure 3.11   Under-the-counter water purifiers work fine, as long as the water is running. This unit will be installed under the sink and can also be used with a hand pump, shown in the foreground.

killed by boiling, it will not be killed by chlorine or bleach-treated water. "Purifiers" (as opposed to filters), by U.S. federal guidelines, are required to protect against all three types of disease organisms, including viruses.

It is probably a good idea to attach a permanent water purifier to your water line under the kitchen sink. However, you may want to get a portable unit in case no water is coming out of your tap and you are using stored water. Water purifiers come as portable units ($75.00, Figure 3.10), under-the-counter units ($200–500, Figure 3.11), and even an under-the-counter unit that can be used with a hand-pumped emergency preparedness kit with a $150.00 adapter if your tap water stops running.[3] With these units, no boiling or chemical treatment is required. Be sure to get extra cartridges when you buy your unit. The manufacturer will specify how many gallons can be purified with each cartridge.

Boiling

Boiling is a common approach to treating water. You must bring the water to a rapid boil for at least 10 minutes (15 in higher altitudes)—

Figure 3.12 Boiling water will kill pathogens that cause disease but will not remove contaminants that water purifiers do.

and this can use up a lot of precious cooking fuel. Boiling water will also leave a flat taste that can be improved by adding a pinch of salt and aerating the water by pouring it back and forth between two containers. Keep in mind that some water will evaporate. Let the water cool before drinking. Though boiling will get rid of bacteria and pathogens, it will not remove pesticides, insecticides, heavy metals, salts, most other chemicals, and radioactive fallout. Only filtering the water through a quality purifier will get out contaminants. (Figure 3.12).

Chemical Treatments

Water can be treated chemically to remove dangerous bacteria and viruses, but not Crypto, Giardia, or other larger pathogens. As with boiling, chemical treating will not remove pesticides, insecticides, and other chemical pollutants. Chlorine, in the form of fresh (less than one year old) regular household bleach (5.25% solution), is the most common chemical added to the water. Be sure no soap, phosphate, or scent is added. Some containers warn, "Not For Personal Use." You can disregard these warnings if the label states sodium hypochlorite is the only active ingredient and if you use only the small quantities in these instructions.

Use 8 drops per gallon for clear water, 16 drops for cloudy (for 55 gallon use 1 oz. if clear, 2 oz. if cloudy). The water will have a slight chlorine odor at first, but let it stand for at least 30 minutes. It may seem strange to be adding chlorine to your drinking water, but remember that's what they are doing at your local water treatment plant (Figure 3.13).

Figure 3.13 Common household bleach (unscented) can effectively treat water. Bleach contains the same chlorine that is used to treat city water.

Treating water with household bleach*
(5.25% sodium hypochlorite unscented)

Water Quantity	Water Condition	Bleach
1 quart	Clear	2 drops
1 quart	Cloudy	4 drops
1 gallon	Clear	8 drops
1 gallon	Cloudy	16 drops
5 gallons	Clear	½ teaspoon
5 gallons	Cloudy	1 teaspoons
55 gallons	Clear	1 ounce
55 gallons	Cloudy	2 ounces

*Use bleach less than one year old!

You can also purchase tablets that are specifically made for treating water wherever camping goods are sold. These are usually a 2% tincture of iodine. Just follow the instructions on the bottle. You could buy tincture of iodine (2%) and use 3–5 drops per gallon. However, iodine usually leaves a taste (you can add a little Kool-Aid) and odor and should not be used by nursing or pregnant women or people with thyroid problems. Also, it can be rather expensive treating large amounts of water with iodine. Iodine, like chlorine, is not effective against Crypto (Figure 3.14).

Figure 3.14   Iodine tablets can also treat water but leave an unpleasant taste and smell.

More Rigorous Purification Methods for Radioactive Fallout

While the three methods described above will remove only microbes from water, the following two purification methods will remove other chemicals, and radioactive dust and dirt, called radioactive fallout. Filtering will also remove radioactive fallout. Water itself cannot become radioactive, but it can be contaminated by radioactive fallout. It is unsafe to drink water that contains radioactive fallout.

DISTILLATION

Distillation involves boiling water and then collecting the vapor that condenses back to water. The condensed vapor will not include salt and other impurities. To distill, fill a pot halfway with water. Tie a cup to the handle on the pot's lid so that the cup will hang right-side-up when the lid is upside-down (make sure the cup is not dangling into the water) and boil the water for 20 minutes. The water that drips from the lid into the cup is distilled.

FALLOUT FILTERS

To make a fallout filter, punch holes in the bottom of a large bucket, and put a layer of gravel in the bucket about 1½ inches high. Cover the gravel with a towel cut in a circle slightly larger than the bucket. Cover the towel with a soil (6"–12"), place the filter over a large container, and pour contaminated water through. Then, disinfect the filtered water using one of the methods described above. Change the soil in your filter after every 50 quarts of water.

Wells

Many people do not rely on central water systems but, rather, have their own wells (Figure 3.15). Unless there is a major environmental disaster nearby that pollutes the underground water table, this water should be fine. The problem is getting the water out of the ground without electricity. You can get a generator that you can hook to your well pump. Just be sure you know how to hook it up and that the generator has the capacity to drive the pump (many of which are 220 volts).

There are small buckets available that allow you to take the pump out and lower a small bucket to manually draw out the water but this can be slow and exhausting (unless you have energetic kids around). However, pulling a submersible pump can be a major chore. There are manual pumping systems that are easier and systems that can use a pump that can run off solar or wind power.[4] Also it may be a good idea to replace your existing 50–100 gallon pressurized well storage tank with a larger one so that each time you fire up the pump it will store more water.

Figure 3.15   Wells are a good source of water if you have electricity to power
the pump.

NOTES

1 Watertanks.com: www.watertanks.com, 1-877-420-8657. They have tanks from 55 to
   50,000 gallons.
2 Jade Mountain, 1-800-442-1972, www.jademountain.com. The Survival Center, 1-800-
   321-2900, http://survivalcenter.com
3 General Ecology, Inc., 1-800-441-8166, www.general-ecology.com and Epic Water
   Systems, 1-800-474-3742, www.epicwater.com
4 Jade Mountain, 1-800-442-1972, www.jademountian.com. The Survival Center, 1-800-
   321-2900, http://survivalcenter.com

CHECKLIST FOR WATER

- ❑ Water
- ❑ Water containers
- ❑ Aerobic oxygen (optional)
- ❑ Water pumps (manual or battery-operated)
- ❑ Iodine—2% (optional)
- ❑ Water purifier with extra cartridges
- ❑ Bleach (5.25 % sodium hypochlorite unscented, less than 1 year old)

HEATING

"Preparedness is a little like plumbing. No one wants to think about it until something goes wrong, and then no one can think about anything else until it gets fixed."

—Kay C. Goss, FEMA's Associate Director for Preparedness

THE PROBLEM

In areas where the weather will likely be cold, alternative heat must be provided in case there is a loss of electrical power or an interruption in coal, oil, or gas deliveries. The concept that losing power in cold climates can threaten lives was brought home on January 8, 1998, when parts of the United States and Canada lost power for several weeks in an ice storm. Emergency efforts were strained trying to rescue people trapped in their homes in freezing conditions. Many had resorted to burning valuable furniture in energy-inefficient fireplaces. Three to five million people were without power, some for as long as 22 days—all in freezing conditions. Twenty-two people died as a result of the storm.

Should disaster-related failures cause large areas of countries in cold climates to lose the ability to provide heat to their citizens, people may not be able to rely on the usual emergency efforts to help them. We must go into this event assuming we will have ourselves, our neighbors, and our immediate community to help.

Even if you have heating fuel, a loss of electrical power will disable our central heating systems, most of which will not operate without power. Therefore, true disaster preparedness includes for every person living in a cold climate, enough fuel, and a nonelectric heating system, to keep warm through at least several weeks of power outages or fuel delivery disruptions. In extremely cold climates, where life can be threatened, we would even recommend a second back-up system (two kerosene heaters, two propane heaters, etc.) should your main alternative system experience problems.

Another problem that may occur if we lose heat and/or water in the middle of winter is that the pipes can freeze and burst. If pipes are not already wrapped, wrap them in insulation or layers of old newspapers. Cover the newspapers with plastic to keep out moisture. Let faucets drip a little to avoid freezing. Know how to shut off water valves. Because of the threat of fire, never use a blow torch or open flames to defrost pipes.

When the water is restored and the pipes thaw, flooding in your home may occur if the proper precautions have not been taken. Be sure to turn off the water into your home and to drain the existing water in your system by opening the lowest faucets if your pipes are in danger of freezing. Also be careful in using the water immediately after water service is installed. The first supply coming through the system may be silty or contaminated. Don't use it as drinking water until local officials have declared it safe. Also, be sure you know how to turn off your gas and electrical power.

THE SOLUTIONS

In order to be assured of heat for space heating and cooking, you must find a source of fuel that does not rely on delivery to you from a central source (electricity, natural gas, etc.). That means storing enough fuel, in a secure, safe, and dry area, on your property or otherwise accessible to you, to last as long as the cold weather might last. You do not have to heat the entire home, but enough of it to effectively live in.

And remember, that may be larger than you think. You may be taking in friends and relatives who are in need. So you may want to get ready to know your neighbors, friends, and relatives more closely than you would otherwise. However, looking back on this period, this building of relationships with so many different people, as we prepare for and experience any disaster-related interruptions, may be one of its great blessings. Modern life has driven us apart as a society. We are in our homes watching TV, on the Net, playing with our computers. A study found that when survivors of the years of London bombing during WW II were interviewed 30 years after the bombings, over 60% said that period was the best years of their life. People suffered together, worked together, helped each other, served each other. Life had meaning, where so much of our modern life has become trivialized.

In evaluating your options, and in determining how much fuel to store, you must decide on your "comfort zone" and your "disaster prognosis." "Comfort zone" means how much of your home you plan to heat, for how many hours of the day, to what temperature. The whole house? One room? One day room and one night room? 60 degrees, 65, 70? Heating an entire house, 24 hours a day to 70 degrees will require much more fuel than one large room for 16 hours at 62 degrees. However, the thought of living in one room with all your relatives may convince you that storing enough to heat two rooms is well worth the money. Be aware that storing enough fuel to get through winter may involve large amounts of fuel, which may mean a substantial investment and wise planning for safe secure storage.

"Disaster prognosis" means how long you believe a disaster-related emergency might last, and therefore how much fuel you want to store. However, in situations that may be life-threatening, not just inconvenient, err on the side of caution. If cold weather could threaten your life, not just make you uncomfortable, have enough fuel for the winter.

THE OPTIONS

There are six common sources of fuel that will work in this situation:

- Propane heat
- Generators
- Wood heat
- Kerosene heat
- Oil heat
- Coal stoves
- Solar heat

NOTE: In addition to the above options make sure you have a generous supply of warm clothes, gloves, wool socks, caps, scarves, blankets, and sleeping bags around. Also you may want to keep some rolls of plastic around. You can cover the windows inside and out, and this will cut much heat loss.

Heating Safety

Kerosene heaters may not be legal in your area and should only be used where approved by authorities. Do not use the kitchen oven range to heat your home. In addition to being a fire hazard, it can be a source of toxic fumes. Alternative heaters need their space. Keep anything combustible at least 3 feet away. Make sure your alternative heaters have "tip switches." These "tip switches" are designed to automatically turn off the heater in the event they tip over. Only use the type of fuel recommended by the manufacturer, and follow suggested guidelines.

Never refill a space heater while it is operating or still hot. Refuel heaters only outdoors. Make sure wood stoves are properly installed and at least 3 feet away from combustible materials. Ensure they have the proper floor support and adequate ventilation. Use a glass or metal screen in front of your fireplace to prevent sparks from igniting nearby carpets, furniture, or other combustible items.

When using these alternate fuels be sure you have three safety devices:

- Fire extinguisher
- Battery-operated or photoelectric smoke detector
- Battery-operated or photoelectric carbon monoxide detector

(Kerosene stoves are safe when used as instructed, but all open flames use oxygen and give off carbon monoxide. And all open flames have inherent fire risks.)

Propane

Propane gas (also called LP gas) is perhaps one of the best alternatives as it is often used to heat homes in normal conditions. Propane should not be confused with NG gas (or natural gas). Propane is stored on your property in large tanks (often buried in the ground; Figures 4.1, 4.2). NG is piped into your home from a central source, which might be affected by a disaster. The advantages of propane are many. It is a clean, efficient source of heat that can easily be stored in large volumes (5–1,500 gallons) in buried or above-ground tanks that are provided at a nominal charge from the gas supplier. The larger tanks are enough for almost any winter. It can be used as your sole

Figure 4.1 Large propane tanks like this can hold 500–1000 gallons which can last a full winter in many areas. There are above-ground or in-ground tanks.

Figure 4.2   Once buried, the propane tank is barely noticeable.

source of heat, both in normal and electrically challenged times. Its only real disadvantage is that burying or storing gas in above-ground tanks may not work in every home.

If you have central propane heating, your heat may not work if the power is out as these central units require some power for blowers and ignition systems. To solve this, there are two alternatives. Check with the heating manufacturer to see if you can hook your system in to a small generator to provide this power. You can even hook up propane generators ($4,000–10,000) or propane refrigerators[1] to your propane tanks.

Or perhaps the best option is to install small wall propane heaters that do not require electricity (Figure 4.3). These can be installed in place of, or in addition to, the central propane system. These small units can be installed for $300–500 each and can heat one room or several if strategically placed. They do not require any electricity and with several of these and 500 to 1000 gallons of propane in your tank, your heating problem is solved. Unvented propane spot heaters can easily be installed in any room except the bedroom. In bedrooms most states require using a small (6") vent pipe to the outside. You can even buy units that look like fireplaces with gas logs. You may

Figure 4.3   These propane wall heaters require no electricity, as will a propane furnace. Wall heaters can produce up to 30,000 BTUs—enough for a small house or several rooms.

Figure 4.4   There are also small portable propane heaters. Avoid the ones that use the small cylinders and get the ones that can hook to 5-gallon tanks.

also want to consider adding energy-efficient propane gas logs to your existing fireplace. There are also small portable propane heaters. Avoid the ones that use the small cylinders; instead, get the ones that can hook to 5-gallon tanks (Figure 4.4).

Generators

Many people, when they think about power outages, immediately think about getting a generator. This is a good idea to power some appliances (lights, freezer, TV, washer, fans, blowers for central heating systems or gas hot water heaters, etc.). However, using a generator to create heat, either for cooking or space heating, requires a large generator and a large supply of fuel. This is a very expensive option, often requiring large storage tanks and expensive generators professionally wired into your electrical system. Even then, it is an inefficient way to heat a home. (For more, see Generators in the Lighting chapter.)

Wood Heat

Wood heat is a pleasant and inexpensive option, though not practical in every situation. Its advantages are that in many areas wood is abundant, inexpensive, and safe to store. It is pleasant, healthy (if moisture is added to the air), and obtainable in some areas for free by homeowners with the proper equipment. And once a wood heating system is installed, it can be a source of ongoing enjoyment and wise contingency planning. However, it has several disadvantages. It is not practical in all homes (New York City co-ops may object to wood stoves retrofitted into their buildings), it is expensive to install, and the heating source cannot be moved from room to room.

You can have several cords delivered to your property and available at the beginning of each winter. Be sure that it is good dry hardwood, the proper length for your stove or fireplace, and can be stored in a secure, dry area where theft will not be a problem. A cord (4' feet wide by 4' tall by 8' long, or 128 cubic feet) can cost anywhere from $40–120, depending on location and the quality of the wood and whether it is stacked neatly or dumped (Figure 4.5). Wood pellet stoves are also a possibility. These use small processed wood pellets instead of chopped wood. These can be very efficient, but be sure you store enough pellets.

Figure 4.5　　If you plan to use wood, be sure you store enough for the winter.

It is difficult to give general rules as to how much wood you will need. It varies according to the stove, the wood, the size and outside air infiltration of the space being heated. The best thing to do is to test your stove or fireplace and then calculate from there how much wood you will need.

If you are depending on wood as your heat, also have the following:

- A chainsaw with fuel
- A secure storage area
- Kindling and fire starters
- A gas jet in your fireplace to start the fire (optional)
- Newspaper
- Wooden, waterproof matches
- Log carrying bag
- A good grate
- Fireplace heat deflector (optional, but a good idea with energy-inefficient fireplaces)
- Fireplace tools (brush, shovel, bellows, poker, etc.)
- Battery operated smoke detector

- Battery operated carbon monoxide detector
- Fire extinguisher

FIREPLACES

There are several options as to what type of wood heater to use. However, be careful in thinking that your existing fireplace will provide much heat. Typical wood fireplaces in residences are mostly decorative and 80–100% of the heat goes up the chimney. Some even make the house colder as they burn by drawing cold air into the home to feed the fire with air. Energy-efficient inserts and heat reflectors can be installed in these types of fireplaces to increase their efficiency, but typical wood-burning fireplaces are still not an effective way to heat the home. However, you may add a very energy-efficient set of propane gas logs to your existing fireplace to make it a viable alternative. These logs are 80–95% efficient compared to the 0–20% of most fireplaces.

You can get energy-efficient fireplaces or inserts that work much better. Two companies make energy-efficient built-in fireplaces[2] (Figure 4.6). Units cost from $1,200 to 2,000 plus installation. Instead

Figure 4.6   This energy-efficient wood fireplace is 50–70% efficient compared to 0–20% efficiency of standard residential wood fireplaces.

of 0–20% efficiency, these units can give 50–70% efficiency. The units have optional electric blowers that can spread the heat around, but these require electricity, which may require a generator if the power is off. However, these more efficient units must be either built into a new home or installed after removing an existing unit. This can be very expensive or impossible, in which case going to a wood stove is advised for wood heat.

WOOD STOVES

Wood stoves are by far the preferred way to heat with wood. They are less expensive, easier to install, more efficient, and more readily available than energy-efficient wood fireplaces (Figure 4.7). There are some excellent energy-efficient wood stoves that can be installed in most existing homes. Be sure you get a serious wood stove, not one

Figure 4.7   A good energy-efficient wood stove can heat several rooms or a small house. Some only need to be refueled every 12–24 hours.

made mostly for decorative purposes. Compare pricing, features, efficiency ratings, how much wood they burn, etc. Get an efficient stove that you can damp down and burn though the night, so it only requires stoking in the morning. There are even small portable wood stoves on the market that can be moved with a small 3–4" flue pipe poked out a window[3] (Figure 4.8). However, these are best saved for emergency backup, as they burn a lot of wood and usually will only heat a small room.

If you are having a wood stove retrofitted into your home, either follow the instructions carefully or leave it to a professional. The last

Figure 4.8   Small, portable wood camp stoves require only a 4" flue and can be moved.

thing you want is to proudly walk over to your wood stove when the power goes off, light it up, and burn your house down. And remember, the local fire department may have a somewhat slower response rate in the early stages of an emergency.

WOOD STOVE ACCESSORIES

Should you decide to go with a wood stove, you may want to consider several options that can be fitted onto some wood stoves. There are water heater units that will allow you to heat your water as you heat your house. Also there are oven units, often inserted into the flue pipe, that will allow you to bake with the waste heat going up the flue. There are even heat exchangers, which capture the heat going up the flue, that can be inserted into your flue pipe to capture the waste heat.

Kerosene

In the past, kerosene was seen as a smelly, dirty way to heat a home. However, in recent years odorless, sootless kerosene heaters have made kerosene heating a viable alternative (Figure 4.9). As with all open flame heating, there is a greater fire risk, but this is negligible if you follow the manufacturer's safety instructions. If used properly, they are safe, inexpensive, efficient, and give out minimal odor. The advantage of a portable kerosene heater is that it can be moved from room to room as your needs change during the day. It can be placed in the living room during the day, in the kitchen at meals, and in the bedroom at night. The disadvantage is that it cannot provide whole house heating without operating units in many rooms, and fuel storage can be a problem.

Be sure to check the specification sheet with the heater to see how much kerosene it burns per hour. Then multiply how many hours each day by number of days you want to store to calculate your fuel needs. For instance, a typical portable kerosene heater produces 23,000 BTUs by burning 1 gallon every 6 to 8 hours. So if you use it 16 hours a day, you will need 2–3 gallons a day. This may not seem like a lot, but if you have four months of winter you will need 240–360 gallons. That's alot of 5-gallon cans or one large storage tank. And that only fuels one heater for two-thirds of the day. Storing flam-

Figure 4.9   Kerosene heaters are safe, odorless, and can be moved from room to room. Be sure to follow manufacturer's safety instructions and directions to avoid fire and burns.

mable fuels should always be done away from the house and not in attached garages or sheds. Most manufacturers recommend that the kerosene be less than 6–12 months old, so you may not want to start storing until late summer (Figure 4.10).

Figure 4.10   This is enough kerosene to run one heater, 24 hours per day for only 20 days. You will need much more to get through the winter in many areas.

Oil Heat

Many older homes are heated with heating oil through central furnaces. The oil is stored in large tanks placed outside the house, usually above ground (Figure 4.11). Some of these will work without electricity; others won't. The older the unit, the more likely it is to work. The older units were gravity-fed. New units often use electrical pumps and switches. Also, the older floor units did not use electrical blowers but rather simply allowed the heat to rise. Be sure to test your unit. Turn it on and the power off and see what happens.

There are free-standing oil stoves that can be retrofitted in homes, much like a wood stove (Figure 4.12). These can create up to 30,000 BTU output, yet they use less than ¼ gallon of oil per hour at the highest setting.[3] These are often gravity-fed, requiring no power. They cost $1,000–2,000.

Figure 4.11   Heating oil is stored in large tanks and is often gravity fed to heater.

Figure 4.12   Free-standing oil stoves can be retrofitted into homes, much like a wood stove. Many require no electricity.

Coal Stoves

In the past, coal was a common source of home heating fuel. Coal use in homes has died out in the United States, but now there is a new type of coal stove on the market that can be installed in any home just like a wood stove. In fact, it is easier than adding a wood stove in that it only requires a 6" vent that can vent directly out any wall or roof (Figure 4.13).

These stoves use low-cost anthracite coal that is available in most areas. They are odorless and smokeless. They are very energy-efficient and burn twice as hot as wood. They can heat a three-bedroom house and are easy to operate, many with gravity hopper systems. Many can burn for 24 hours and can be thermostatically controlled.

Figure 4.13　　Coal stoves can be added to any home. These newer models burn twice as hot as wood and only need to be refueled every 24 hours.

Solar Power

Solar power may definitely be a viable option to heat your water, at times even your home, as well as create electricity in the event of an infrastructure failure. We will not spend much time here on solar power, not because we do not feel it is a good way to go, but rather because its expense to heat a home makes it infeasible for most people. Also, solar power works in relationship with the amount of available sunlight. Heating or creating electricity with solar power in the middle of winter in New Mexico will be quite different than in the Seattle area.

SOLAR WATER HEATERS

Heating your hot water with solar power is more affordable than heating your home (Figure 4.14). Several panels on the roof, for several thousand dollars, will do it in most areas. However, if the water system is not working, you may not have pressurized water, so these will be of little use.[3]

Figure 4.14   Solar panels can heat your water but remember it takes water pressure to work.

SOLAR SPACE HEATING

Heating a home with solar power can cost tens of thousands of dollars and may not be feasible for many retrofits. Some houses are designed to orient toward the winter sun and capture the heat in masonry, adobe, or brick mass walls inside the house that act as heat sinks. These homes are called passive solar, and though adding on a passive solar room is possible, for the most part homes must be designed and built to be passive solar.

An active solar system involves capturing the sun's energy with solar panels, usually on the roof, and then using something like water to bring the sun's heat into mass storage areas. Though this too can be retrofitted on some homes, it is expensive.[4]

PHOTOVOLTAICS (SOLAR ELECTRICITY)

Photovoltaic cells can now create electricity from sunlight (Figure 4.15). These are available and practical, though to install a large enough system to take your entire home off the grid (ah the grid, the poor old maligned grid) can cost thousands of dollars. You can get a small system of cells, inverters and storage batteries for around $1,000 that in many areas will create enough electricity to run lights, TVs, and radios. This may be a good option as a backup in the event we lose the grid for a period of time. At least you will have lights and can use small appliances.[5]

SOLAR OVENS

Often your heating source can also serve as your stove. There are some very inexpensive solar ovens on the market that can cook a meal in minutes at no cost just by sitting in the sun.[6]

Having said this about solar power, perhaps the awareness of the vulnerability of centralized power systems will steer us in the direction of renewable, non-polluting energy sources (solar, wind, wave, hydro, etc.). Once we realize how vulnerable we are with large centralized systems, we will begin to see the wisdom of a smaller decentralized system. If we have a wind or solar system in our houses generating a minimum level of electricity, we will never be prone to system failures

Figure 4.15   Photovoltaic cells such as these can turn sunlight into electricity. You can power a light or an entire house.

again. We would have free, constant non-polluting energy forever. The technology is there, but as yet the will is not there to develop these. A picture of the Los Angeles rooftops in the 1930s shows almost 20% of the homes with solar water panels. They disappeared as the electric and gas companies paid homeowners to remove them and hook into their centralized systems.

NOTES

[1] Heat-N-Glo of Savage, MN, 1-800-669-4328, www.heatnglo.com and Majestic
Fireplaces of Huntington, IN, 1-800-227-8683, www.vermontcastings.com
[2] Riley Stove Company of Townsend, MT, 406-266-5525
[3] Jade Mountain, 1-800-442-1975, www.jademountain.com (Be sure to mention
#241) and The Survival Center, 1-800-321-2900, http://survivalcenter.com
[4] Ibid
[5] Ibid
[6] Ibid

CHECKLIST FOR HEATING

Alternative Heating

❑ Propane heat
❑ Generators
❑ Wood heat
❑ Kerosene heat
❑ Oil heat
❑ Coal stoves
❑ Solar heat

Fuel

❑ Propane
❑ Kerosene
❑ Wood
❑ Oil
❑ Coal
❑ Gasoline (for generator if needed)

Other

❑ Warm clothes
❑ Gloves
❑ Wool socks
❑ Caps

❏ Scarves
❏ Blankets
❏ Sleeping bags

For Wood Heating

❏ A chainsaw with fuel
❏ A secure storage area
❏ Kindling and fire starters
❏ A gas jet in your fireplace to start the fire (optional), newspaper
❏ Wooden, waterproof matches
❏ Log carrying bag
❏ A good grate
❏ Fireplace heat deflector (optional, but a good idea with energy-inefficient fireplaces)
❏ Fireplace tools (brush, shovel, bellows, poker, etc.)

Safety

❏ Fire extinguisher
❏ Battery-operated or photoelectric smoke detector
❏ Battery-operated or photoelectric carbon monoxide detector
❏ *The Complete Y2K Home Preparation Guide*

LIGHTING WITHOUT ELECTRICITY

"The biggest problems and opportunities are not going to be food storage, debugging code, or power outages, but how people react to the situation: how we treat each other; how much we help each other through this; what kind of creative, appropriate responses we meet the challenge with will determine whether we build and bring together our local communities or whether things degenerate into mob rule."
                                                        —Michael Connolly, WizCity

THE PROBLEM

Should there be a temporary lapse in electrical power, alternative sources of lighting must be provided for in advance. Lighting is essential. If your house is plunged into darkness at 5:30 each afternoon, chances are your mood will follow. Acquiring emergency lighting before the event, is relatively inexpensive and easy. After the event, it becomes very difficult, perhaps impossible (try to find a candle or batteries after they have announced a hurricane is heading your way!).

As with cooking, alternative methods of lighting are inexpensive and easily obtainable. However, do not plan as you would for a three to five day event. This means do not depend on battery-operated lighting, unless you plan to use batteries rechargeable by either the sun or by cranking up a generator. However, using your generator to recharge batteries is like cutting butter with a chainsaw, and solar rechargers are slow and depend on available sunlight.

Recommended sources of alternative lighting include:

- Generators
- Solar lantern, flashlights, and electrical systems
- Gas lanterns
- Kerosene lanterns
- Candles
- Battery-operated lanterns and flashlights

THE SOLUTIONS

Generators

We have listed generators first not because everyone should buy one or because they are the recommended source of alternative lighting (they're not always), but because many people, when they think about power outages, immediately think about getting a generator (Figure 5.1). This may be a good idea to power some appliances (lights, TV, washer, fans, blowers for central heating systems or gas hot water heaters, etc.).

If you can afford it, buying a generator to provide lighting makes some sense. However, the other methods listed above will also work at a fraction of the cost. Small generators can be used to watch a video, play music, start your washing machine, charge a battery, run a computer, power a TV, and many other things you would never think of until you were without power. You simply start the generator and plug appliances and lights directly into it, or more likely, since generators should never be run in a living area, into extension cords plugged into the generator. Be sure to use heavy-duty extension cords, not the light-weight ones meant for one or two lights. Also, never run the generator indoors or in the basement as the fumes are dangerous. If you run it in a garage, be sure to leave a door or window open to the outside for ventilation.

Figure 5.1   A small generator can supply all your lighting needs (plus a TV or radio) while using much less fuel than the larger units. Be sure to get extra spark plugs, lubricating oil, and oil filters.

If you are considering buying a generator, give it a lot of thought and don't assume bigger is better. The larger the generator, the more fuel it will demand. If disruptions last for an extended period, you would need to store a large amount of fuel. A smaller generator may well serve your needs, cost less, and require less fuel than a larger unit.

You can buy a 1500–1850-watt generator for around $400 at any home center. This will be more than enough to run lighting and small appliances. You can even run your washing machine or gas dryer. It would probably run your refrigerator, but when cold foods are available in the stores, your own power is probably not far behind. A $700 Honda generator that has only 650–1000 watts but uses less fuel than the 1500–1850-watt generators (only one gallon per 8–18 hours) is much quieter and will last much longer.

You can jump up to 5000+ watts and power your whole house, but these cost a good deal more and take a lot of fuel. You can wire them directly into your electrical box, but you should have this done professionally as it is very dangerous. If done incorrectly, you can not only ruin your electrical system and generator, but also potentially electrocute power company linemen working on the lines. We do not recommend this approach unless money is not a concern and you are determined to live as near as normal life as possible no matter what happens.

In choosing a generator you can also choose from several different fuel sources. Some generators can even run on several different fuels, but again, these are more expensive. Be sure to check the specs and see how long each generator will run on a gallon of fuel. A 650-watt gas generator will run 8 hours on 1 gallon. A 6000-watt gas generator will need 6 gallons for the same hour. You will need six times more fuel for the 6000-watt over the 650-watt—not a good idea unless you need the added wattage (Figure 5.2).

Propane is one possibility. Propane generators cost $3000 and up but are very quiet, fuel-efficient, and dependable. You can store large volumes of propane (LP gas) in below- and above-ground (5-1000 gallons) tanks. Most local propane suppliers will rent you tanks at a nominal yearly fee. Propane generators are expensive but never clog. They

Figure 5.2   Plastic sheds like these make excellent storage for fuel. Be sure it is kept a safe distance from the house.

are the cleanest and do not smell. A large quantity of the fuel is easy to store and does not age after a year, as will gasoline and diesel. There are even converters that can turn a gasoline generator into a propane generator for around $300.

Gasoline is the most common and least expensive type of generator. It also requires more fuel to create the same wattage as produced by either diesel or propane. Gasoline may start to degrade after one year, unless a gas extender additive is added. Gas generators are available from 500 watts upward. They are the most common generators and can be found at any home center or power generator dealer. Some are quite loud, so check the decibel ratings (Honda has some very quiet generators). It is best to buy a generator with "full pressure lubrication." These will last much longer than "splash lubrication." Also try to get a "brushless" unit.

Diesel is more dependable, and diesel fuel will last longer than gas, but these generators cost more and diesel fuel may be harder to get in an emergency. Diesel generators may be noisier, but they are very dependable and more efficient than gas. They may be somewhat harder to start in cold weather.

If you buy a generator, learn how to work it before you need it. You don't want to be sitting in your garage when the power goes out reading the owner's manual with a flashlight and trying to fill it with gas. Start your generator every two months to keep openings clear. After it has run a few minutes, turn off the gas line from the tank (if there is one) and let the generator run out of gas. This will help the lines from clogging. Always have several extra spark plugs available if your generator uses them. Also keep the fuel tank and all storage tanks topped off so they do not sweat and drip water in the fuel. Shake your generator a little before starting it to mix any water that may have gotten in the tank. You may want to add a gas stabilizer or saver to the tank as well when you store the gas. As always, store your fuel in a safe, dry, secure location but never indoors, in the garage, or attached to the house. Keep a fire extinguisher nearby and a battery-operated fire alarm in the storage area.

GENERATOR SAFETY

Follow the manufacturer's instructions and guidelines when using generators. Use a generator or other fuel-powered machine outside the home. Carbon monoxide fumes are odorless and can quickly overwhelm you indoors. Use the appropriate size and type of power cords to carry the electric load. Overloaded cords can overheat and cause fires. Never run cords under rugs or carpets where heat might build up or damage to a cord may go unnoticed. Never connect generators to another power source such as power lines. The reverse flow of electricity or "back feed" can electrocute an unsuspecting utility worker.

Solar Lanterns and Flashlights

In the last 20 years, solar technology has developed to the point that now solar lanterns, flashlights, radios, water pumps, etc., are all viable alternative emergency equipment (Figure 5.3). Solar lanterns now cost around $100 (Figure 5.4). These units will provide light for 8 hours on a full charge (full charge is 8 hours in direct sunlight; longer on cloudy

Figure 5.3   All of these lighting devices are solar powered.

Figure 5.4   Solar lanterns are an excellent choice. They will charge even on cloudy days and will burn 8 hours on a full charge.

or hazy days or wintertime). They have a solar cell that you put in the sun (or toward the sun on cloudy days) and this charges the battery in the unit. After the initial purchase, your lighting is free and non-pollutting forever. You do not need batteries or to store dangerous fuel.

There are also solar-powered flashlights, radios, and battery chargers that we recommend. Another thing to consider is to buy several of the solar outdoor pathway lamps. These are rather inexpensive (around $50 at any home center), and several brought inside every night can provide ambient lighting (Figure 5.5). There are even solar-powered flood lights with cells placed on your roof (Figure 5.6).

You can also now buy small solar electrical systems. These involve solar cells (photovoltaics) usually installed on the roof, toward the sun. These cells create electricity, which is stored in batteries. You can then attach various 12-volt lights and appliances (radios, TVs, videos, fans, water pumps, etc.) to these batteries and presto—free, clean energy. Small systems that will power several lights or appliances cost around $1,000–2,000. Larger systems that can power everything in

Figure 5.5   These solar lights are made for outdoor walkways but can be brought inside for ambient lighting.

Figure 5.6   Even standard floodlights like these now come in solar units.

your home can cost tens of thousands of dollars. Wind generators are also viable if you live where there is a lot of wind.[1]

Gas Lanterns

Gas lanterns have been the favorite of campers and fishermen for decades. With these lanterns you must pump up the tank with a built-in plunger for a few pumps to put the fuel under pressure (Figure 5.7). Recently, propane and butane models have been introduced, but these require that you have a supply of small canisters (unless you can get one that hooks to a larger tank) (Figure 5.8). These lanterns provide a very bright light (the same as a 200-watt bulb) and even give off enough heat to take a chill off the room if the weather is not too cold. They are fairly efficient.

A two-mantle lantern will burn for 40 hours on a gallon of fuel. If you use it for four hours per night, you will need 3–4 gallons per month. (A two-burner propane will burn 4.5 hours on a 16 oz canister.) The dual fuel models can burn either white gas or car gas and are

Figure 5.7   These hand-pumped, two-mantle, dual-fuel camp lanterns can burn white or standard gasoline. They give off 200 watts of light but make an annoying hissing sound. There is now a new kerosene version available.

Figure 5.8   These propane gas lanterns work well but require a supply of small propane canisters. Some units can be hooked to larger 5-gallon tanks. Be sure to have a supply of extra mantles. Also cook stoves and small heaters are available.

recommended for any emergency. Be sure you have a good supply of extra wicks, as they break often. One major drawback with these lanterns is they make a hissing noise. This is very irritating after an hour reading a book so you may prefer the quiet of kerosene, candles, or solar lighting. You can keep the bright dual-mantle lantern for when you need bright lighting. As always, store your fuel in a safe, dry, secure location but never indoors, in the garage or attached to the house. Keep a fire extinguisher nearby and a battery-operated fire alarm in the storage area.

Two mantle gas lantern fuel consumption

Period	Fuel Consumed per 4 Hours
Day	¼ Quart
Week	3 Quarts
Month	3 Gallons
Year	36 Gallons

Kerosene Lanterns

Kerosene lamps and lanterns of all styles have been popular for centuries (Figure 5.9). We've seen them in every western we've ever

Figure 5.9 Old-fashioned kerosene lamps work well. Keep the wicks trimmed to avoid smoking and be careful—they are a fire hazard. Be sure to get extra wicks.

watched. For the most part they are simple devices with wicks, globes, and a container for the kerosene. They come in everything from the railroad swinging lanterns to ornate parlor lamps (Figure 5.10).

Given today's technology, a kerosene lantern seems a bit old-fashioned and out of place. Kerosene lanterns are an effective and fairly safe lighting source. There are now scented lamp oils which replace kerosene (Figure 5.11). This lamp oil is generally available in retail stores. Make sure the oil is approved for use in your lamp.

Kerosene lamps and lanterns are a good source of dependable, inexpensive lighting. They give off a slight odor (you can add scents) and will smoke if the wick is not trimmed periodically. Also, remember to never grab the globe at the top while the lamp is burning. It's hot!

There are kerosene lamps on the market, Aladdin, that works better than all the rest (Figure 5.12). It burns brighter and with no smell.[2] They are beautiful lamps. However, you will need several extra mantles as they are rather delicate.

There is a difference in lighting quantity and quality, and the traditional kerosene lantern is quite dim when compared to the two-mantle gas lantern (except for the mantle kerosene lamps like Aladdin, Petromax, or Butterfly). The light output of a kerosene lantern is com-

Figure 5.10   These kerosene "railroad" lanterns work great outside, where wind is an issue.

Figure 5.11   Lamps using scented oils have become popular recently.

Figure 5.12   Alladin Lamps are kerosene lamps that burn much brighter than standard kerosene lamps. Be sure you have extra mantles—they're fragile.

parable to a 40- to 60-watt light bulb. The gas lantern and newer kerosene mantle lamps are equivalent to a 200-watt bulb. However, traditional kerosene lamps that use wicks burn only about ¼ the fuel of the gas lanterns.

As a rule of thumb, the typical kerosene lantern burns approximately 1 ounce of fuel per hour. Burning at the rate of 4 hours each day means one lamp would burn 1 gallon per month. A gas lantern needs 3–4 gallons per month. As always, store your fuel in a safe, dry, secure location but never indoors, in the garage, or structure attached to the house. Keep a fire extinguisher nearby and a battery-operated fire alarm in the storage area. Remember to add an additive to your gas to extend its life.

Kerosene lantern fuel consumption

Period	Fuel Consumed per 4 Hours
Day	4 oz. (1/4 pint)
Week	1 Quart
Month	1 Gallon
Year	12 Gallons

Candles

Candles are an obvious option for emergency lighting but don't think the decorative wax candles you have lying around the house are the way to go (Figure 5.13). Many of these candles will last no more than an hour or so. In fact, these can be a real fire hazard as they tip over easily and drip. They should not be used for emergency purposes.

There are now emergency candles on the market, no bigger than a chicken pot pie, that will burn for 120 hours. The best options are the candles that were designed for emergencies (Figure 5.14). There are two types of emergency candles available for camping, storage, and emergency purposes. We recommend the type made of hardened wax in a can (Nuwick, $13 for 120 hours) with the capability of utilizing several wicks (usually no more than two is recommended) simultaneously so you can increase the brightness, and even warm food over them.[3] They can boil water in 15 minutes and fry an egg in 5 (Figure 5.15, 5.16).

Figure 5.13 Common household candles like these should be avoided in emergencies. They burn quickly and are a fire hazard.

Figure 5.14 These candles were all made for emergency use. They are long burning and safer when used as directed.

Figure 5.15   These candles will burn for 120 hours and are hard to tip over. You can add an additional wick for more light.

Figure 5.16   This emergency candle can even cook food when two wicks are used.

Battery-operated Flashlights, Lanterns, and More

In an emergency, battery-operated lighting is the first thing that comes to mind (Figure 5.17). In the event of a hurricane or ice storm, where power may be out for only a few days, and then only in one area of the country, these devices would suffice. Where power could be out for much longer periods and over a much broader area, these devices should not be relied on as your sole lighting source. Your batteries

Figure 5.17   It is good to have some battery-operated flashlights around but once the batteries are gone they're useless.

will soon die and supplies run out. New Conventional "D" cell batteries will power a light 5–8 hours. Older batteries have a shorter life and long-life batteries a longer life than conventional. You can get rechargeable, but that assumes you have electricity to recharge them.

You may want to consider solar rechargers, windup Baygen flashlights and radio (you wind a crank and get light or music), or solar lanterns and flashlights.[4] There are even small solar cells that you can place in the sun that will run a radio (Figure 5.18, 5.19).

There is a new product on the market called the PowerZone (Figure 5.20). It is a portable power backup system with build-in lighting. It has a variety of usages. It can power DC loads such as lights. A built-in inverter will run typical low wattage AC loads such as small TV's, laptops, radios, small handtools, cell phones, and indoor lighting. The PowerZone can even jump-start your car. Weighting under 20 pounds, its built-in handle makes it easy to tote along. An internal

Figure 5.18 Windup flashlights and radios are new to the market and require no batteries. You wind for 30 seconds and get 3 minutes of light. Note one on left is also solar powered and has a radio.

Figure 5.19 There are even small solar cells that you can place in the sun that will run a radio.

Figure 5.20 The PowerZone is a portable power backup system that has a variety of usages. It can power DC loads such as lights, run typical AC loads such as TVs, computers, radios, power tools, and indoor lighting.

long-life battery is rechargeable with solar (optional), AC current, or 12-volt DC. Great for emergency backup power.[5]

NOTES

[1] Jade Mountain at 1-800-442-1972 or www.jademountain.com (mention #241)
The Survival Center, 1-800-321-2900, http://survivalcenter.com
[2] Butterfly, 1-770-888-2133 or www.helpyourselfprepare.com
[3] Jade Mountain at 1-800-442-1972 or www.jademountain.com (mention #241)
The Survival Center, 1-800-321-2900, http://survivalcenter.com
[4] SunSolarSystems at 336-775-0240, www.webaccess.net/~sunsolarsystems
[5] Jade Mountain at 1-800-442-1972 or www.jademountain.com (mention #241)
The Survival Center, 1-800-321-2900, http://survivalcenter.com

CHECKLIST FOR LIGHTING

Lighting Alternatives
❏ Generators
❏ Solar lantern, flashlights, and electrical systems
❏ Gas lanterns
❏ Kerosene lanterns
❏ Candles
❏ Battery-operated lanterns and flashlights

Fuel
❏ Kerosene
❏ Gasoline
❏ Batteries
❏ Solar battery recharger
❏ Lamp oil

Other
❏ Extra candle wicks
❏ Extra lantern mantles
❏ Extra kerosene or oil lamp wicks
❏ Extra light bulbs for flashlights, solar lanterns, etc.

Safety
❏ Fire extinguisher
❏ Battery-operated or photoelectric smoke detector
❏ Battery-operated or photoelectric carbon monoxide detector

NON-ELECTRIC COOKING
ALTERNATIVES

"All nations are tied into a system of global economic interdependence as part of the world trading system. Trade, which now represents over one-fifth of the global output, is crucial to the economic development and growth of all national economies. Failures in the electronic systems and devices have the potential to cause supply and service disruptions."
—U.S. Department of Commerce

THE PROBLEM

As with heating and lighting, most all of our cooking equipment is reliant on central sources of power, either electric or gas. If these sources are interrupted, we're eating cold canned foods and raw pasta—a less than appetizing option. Unlike alternative non-electric heating options, the cooking options require a small investment in equipment and a much smaller storage of needed fuels. Except for complex baking recipes, these alternative cooking sources will allow us to eat in near normal manner should we lose power and/or gas. Eating as we are accustomed to has a profound beneficial emotional effect in stressful situations. Therefore, providing a viable cooking alternative is a must.

THE SOLUTIONS

You may feel that providing alternative cooking methods is really not needed. You'll just eat things that don't require cooking. This will work if you are without central utilities for a few days or a week, but anything more than that and you'll kick yourself for not having provided for cooking. (Ever try eating raw instant coffee for your caffeine fix?)

Often your heating source can also serve as your stove. You can boil water or cook eggs on top of a kerosene heater, but it is a definite safety risk and not advised. If you incapacitate your kerosene heater through misuse in the middle of winter you are up the proverbial creek. You can cook on many wood stoves, even add ovens and water heating devices to them, but this can be an awkward way to go—involving the use of rugged cast iron pots and pans and always the danger of burns. Therefore, it is best to provide for cooking separately from heating.

There are several viable cooking equipment alternatives. These include:

- Portable dual-fuel gas stoves
- Portable kerosene stoves
- Portable propane stoves
- Gelled ethanol products
- Wood stoves and fireplaces
- Solar ovens

Be sure all alternative stoves are approved for inside use. Never use a charcoal barbecue grill inside.

NOTE: COOKING AND HEATING WITH GENERATORS

Many people, when they think about power outages, immediately think about getting a generator. This may be a good idea to power some appliances (lights, TV, washer, fans, blowers for central heating systems, or gas hot water heaters, etc.). However, using a generator to create heat, either for cooking or space heating, requires a large generator and a large supply of fuel. This is a very expensive option, often requiring large storage tanks and expensive generators professionally wired into your electrical system. Even then, it is an inefficient way to heat a home or food. (More on Generators in Chapters 4 and 5.)

SAFETY NOTE:

When using these open-flame appliances, be sure you have three safety devices:

- Fire extinguisher
- Battery-operated or photoelectric smoke detector
- Battery-operated or photoelectric carbon monoxide detector

Dual Fuel Stoves

The best option by far is to get the standard Coleman (or similar company) pump-up two-burner camp stove (Figure 6.1). They are cheap, effective, and easy to use. However, do not get the one that only allows the use of white gas. White gas is more expensive and may be hard to find if there is disruption to the refinement or delivery of petroleum products. They now make a dual-fuel model that takes white gas or regular gasoline. You could even siphon gas out of your car to use if necessary. These stoves allow you to cook on two burners at once in a near normal fashion. Avoid the single-

Figure 6.1   Two-burner, pump-up camp stoves like these make most cooking relatively easy. Be sure to get a dual-fuel one which allows you to use gasoline.

burner units made for backpacking (Figure 6.2). You can even get an oven attachment that you place over the flames for baking (keep those fresh brownies coming when everyone starts to get a little restless without TV).

Be sure to store enough fuel to be able to cook for as long as you believe disruption may last. Read the specs to determine how much fuel your stove burns per hour and then calculate from there. Store your fuel in a dry, safe, secure place and never indoors, in the garage, or in anything attached to the house. Gas and diesel are good for one year or less. After that it could gum up equipment (but often it will not). However, if you plan to store for several years, you can get a gas or diesel saver chemical and add it to your gas (Figure 6.3).

Figure 6.2   Avoid the single-burner units made for backpacking.

Figure 6.3   Be sure to use a fuel saver added to your gas if you plan to store it over one year. Also keep containers full so there is no condensation into your gas. You should also use savers for kerosene and diesel. Add the saver immediately after filling can.

Dual Fuel Stoves Fuel Consumption

Period	Fuel Consumed Cooking 3 Meals
Day	2 pints
Week	1.25 gallons
Month	5 gallons
Year	60 gallons

Kerosene Cook Stoves

There are a few cook stoves that use kerosene instead of gasoline (Figure 6.4). They cost about the same, work just as well, and require no periodic hand pumping, as the Coleman camp stoves do. One advantage if you are using a kerosene heating source is that you only need to purchase one type of fuel. They come in one-burner and two-

Figure 6.4 Kerosene stoves are also available but are more cumbersome than gas stoves and most have only one burner.

burner models, are odorless and fuel-efficient. They cook faster than gas stoves. These stoves are safe for indoor use.[1]

Wood Stoves and Fireplaces

People have been cooking on wood stoves and in fireplaces for centuries. If you have either, this is certainly an option (obviously wood stoves are much easier to cook on than fireplaces). Wood stoves can be fitted with water heating units and even ovens that sit on top or are inserted into the flue. You can buy wood cook stoves, with ovens, burners, and water heater and these provide heat as well. If you are planning to use a wood cooking option, you will need to buy a good set of cast iron pots and pans. Normal cookware will not hold up.

Gelled Ethanol Products

Several products are on the market that use a gelled ethanol in a can (similar but better than Sterno—and no, you can't drink it if things get too rough) (Figure 6.5). These products come with small stoves and where they are good for basic cooking, like frying eggs, heating coffee, etc., they really are not made for cooking full meals for a family. Each can will burn for up to four hours and a case of 24 cans costs

Figure 6.5   Gelled ethanol fuels are safe to use indoors and will burn for four hours.

about \$75.[2] These products are relatively odorless and can be safely used indoors. They also can be used for spot heating if needed.

Propane and Butane Camp Stoves and Grills

There are both camp stoves and outside barbecue grills that can be used with bottled propane. However, grills are very inefficient since the flame is far below the pot or pan (Figure 6.6). These can suffice, but they may be somewhat more awkward to use since they may require being hooked to a 5-gallon propane tank (refillable at most convenience stores—if they're open). Never use the barbecue grills indoors.

If you decide to go with a propane or butane camp stove, try to get one that can use a 5-gallon tank and not just the little cylinders used for camping (Figure 6.7). If you use these little tanks, you will need a lot of them.[3] These stoves are excellent for cooking and can be used indoors. Also you may want to see if your propane gas supplier can add a propane stove hooked directly into your large propane tank.

Figure 6.6 Propane or charcoal barbeque grills are inefficient for basic cooking. Never use these grills indoors.

Figure 6.7   These propane and butane camp stoves require small propane canisters which may be hard to find in emergencies.

Standard Propane Ranges

A great option would be to use a standard propane kitchen range, the kind installed in many homes (Figure 6.8). Then you can cook in a normal manner. These are hooked into the large propane underground or above-ground tank that can also supply your heating needs. However, there is one major drawback. Many of these will not work without electricity. They may need electricity for the automatic ignition system. Often the burners will work, but not the oven.

Solar Ovens

Solar ovens are good as a secondary source of alternative cooking but not as your primary source (Figure 6.9). Believe it or not, on a sunny day even a $20 portable solar oven can cook everything from an egg to a pot roast. The quality solar ovens cost about $200-300 and are very effective. The best thing about them is that they cook for free and do not pollute or require fossil fuels. We recommend getting an inexpensive solar oven as a viable secondary alternative on sunny days.[4]

Figure 6.8   Propane kitchen ranges are an excellent option—if they work without electricity. Most will allow you to use the burners, but not the oven, if the power is out.

Figure 6.9   Solar ovens, some costing under $20, can cook an entire meal, including chicken, meatloaf, eggs, cookies, etc.

NOTES

1 Jade Mountain, 1-800-442-1972, www.jademountain.com (Be sure to mention #241) and The Survival Center, 1-800-321-2900, http://survivalcenter.com
2 Alco-Brite Company, 1-801-874-1025
3 Glowmaster Corp., 1-800-272-7008, www.glowmaster.com
4 Butterfly Kerosene Equipment 770-888-2133 or www.helpyourselfprepare.com

CHECKLIST FOR COOKING APPLIANCES

Appliance
- ❏ Portable dual-fuel stoves
- ❏ Portable kerosene stoves
- ❏ Portable propane stoves
- ❏ Gelled ethanol products
- ❏ Wood stoves and fireplaces
- ❏ Solar ovens

Safety
- ❏ Fire extinguisher
- ❏ Battery-operated or photoelectric smoke detector
- ❏ Battery-operated or photoelectric carbon monoxide detector

Fuel (depending on stove)
- ❏ Gasoline
- ❏ Propane (LP bottled gas)
- ❏ Kerosene
- ❏ Gelled ethanol
- ❏ Wood
- ❏ Fuel saver

STAYING CLEAN, HEALTHY, AND SAFE

"Only two things threaten our existence:
A breakdown of society as we know it;
The continuation of society as we know it."
—Jan Blum, Seeds Blum Company

"Mammoth productive facilities with computer minds, cities that engulf the
landscape and pierce the clouds, planes that almost outrace time—these
are awesome, but they cannot be spiritually inspiring. Nothing in our glit-
tering technology can raise man to new heights, because material growth
has been made an end in itself, and, in the absence of moral purpose,
man himself becomes smaller as the works of man becomes bigger.
Gargantuan industry and government, woven into an intricate computer-
ized mechanism, leave the person outside. The sense of participation is lost,
the feeling that ordinary individuals influence important decisions vanish-
es, and man becomes separated and diminished.
"When an individual is no longer a true participant, when he no longer
feels a sense of responsibility to his society, the content of democracy is emptied.
When culture is degraded and vulgarity enthroned, when the social system
does not build security but induces peril, inexorably the individual is impelled
to pull away from a soulless society. This process produces alienation—perhaps
the most pervasive and insidious development in contemporary society."
—Dr. Martin Luther King

THE PROBLEM

As with so many areas of our lives, we do not notice the vast unseen computerized infrastructure that allow most of us in the first world to stay relatively clean, healthy, and safe. There is a vast array of systems that allow clean water to be delivered to our homes, drugs to be available at the stores, hospitals to function, police, emergency, and fire teams to respond, etc. If there is a disruption in water supply, disposing of human waste becomes a problem. If this is not handled properly, disease can quickly spread through a community, with devastating effects. Also, items like toilet paper are often in short supply during emergencies. With a limited ability to keep ourselves and houses clean, disease becomes a greater threat. If the waste treatment plants are not operating properly, then we may be prohibited from flushing our toilets or using other household drains—even if we have water.

Pharmaceutical firms can be vulnerable if there is a disruption in this industry; prescription drugs could become rare, endangering the health and lives of millions. Life-sustaining medical equipment, such as IVs and dialysis machines, must be considered if power is out. Medical facilities may become overtaxed in emergencies.

We need to assume that there is a distinct possibility for some period of time (hopefully days, not months) when we may need to provide for our own health and safety needs, perhaps for the first time in our lives. (See the Red Cross Emergency first aid in back of chapter).

THE SOLUTIONS

Staying Clean

Hunger, thirst, being too hot or cold, or just being dirty and in need of a good hot shower, can make most of us irritable. If the conditions continue for weeks or months, it can lead to depression or anger. In earlier chapters we have discussed how to deal with food, water, and heat; now let's take a look at how to stay clean. Though it may not seem as important an area as these others, after a week with no shower, or no toothpaste, or no toilet paper (a telephone book is a very

Figure 7.1 Store an abundance of toilet paper and other paper products. Each 90-roll box will supply one person for one year.

poor substitute for toilet paper), the importance of cleanliness will come into sharp focus (Figure 7.1).

Bathing

Your ability to bathe normally will depend on the availability of water after the event. It may also depend on the availability of electricity, as many water and waste treatment plants cannot continue to operate normally for more than several days on their emergency generators. Allotting one gallon per day per person in your water storage plans will give each person the opportunity to sponge bathe once a day, and that's about it. Showering, tub bathing, even frequent shampooing, is out of the question on one gallon per day. However, if you want to provide the normal options, more planning, and somewhat more expense, is required. You will need plastic or metal containers for washing dishes, washing clothes, and bathing.

Also, realize that if your central sewer system fails, you may not be allowed to use your drains or toilets until it is declared safe. If water delivery through your normal sources is disrupted and you want to be able to take a hot bath or shower, you will not only have to store much more water but also create an alternative water heating system and showering system as well. There is one inexpensive alternative that requires little water for a reasonable shower: Solar showers are available at most camping goods stores. These are basically black heavy-duty bags that hold 5–10 gallons of water that you can either hang in the sun to heat or pour preheated water into them. You can probably fashion something similar from things around the house, but for $8–15 dollars they are well worth the expense. Then you can just

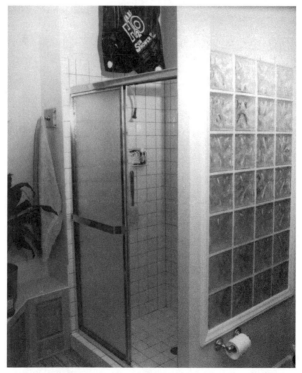

Figure 7.2   Solar showers are inexpensive and easy to use. Just lay or hang the bag in the sun for a few hours and you have a hot shower. This one is hung in a conventional shower for drainage.

hang it in the shower stall as best you can and go from there. The water pressure is a little low, the shower a little short, the water temperature not quite right, but you feel a lot better afterwards than you did before.

Other than these solar showers, you will have to improvise for your bathing needs (Figure 7.2). You can always heat water and pour it in the tub, but this demands a lot of water, a lot of work, and a lot of fuel. If you are using a wood stove, you may want to consider an add-on water heating device, as these will heat water with no waste of extra fuel.

Be sure to have enough soap and shampoo. Dr. Bronner's Soap is an excellent soap that can be purchased at any health food store. Dr. Bronner's has been the favorite of environmentalists and back-to-the-landers for decades. Not only is it biodegradable and will not pollute even if poured into a stream, but it can also be used as soap, shampoo, toothpaste, household detergent, dish soap, shaving cream, denture cleaner, spray for fruits and plants, diaper soap, and laundry soap. It can be diluted, so 2 gallons can last you months. It smells and feels great (Figure 7.3).

Figure 7.3 Biodegradable soaps like Dr. Bronner's do not pollute the environment. They can be used as soap, shampoo, toothpaste, and laundry and dish soap.

Alternative Toilets

You must be prepared if you lose water or your local water and sewer company prohibits anyone from using the drains in their houses. If the waste treatment plant is not working properly, they may need to limit the amount of waste water they can absorb. You may want to consider buying a boat potty for around $60.00 at Walmart or K Mart (Figure 7.4). These are small plastic toilets that store a few gallons of water, to which you add a disinfecting scent, that allows you to flush after every use. There is a holding tank (2–6 gallons) that is removable for disposing of the waste water when it is full. Be sure to store enough of the scented liquid to last. Also, most camping stores sell a toilet seat that fits over a 5-gallon bucket, and you fit a plastic bag into the bucket. Primitive, smelly, but it will work (Figure 7.5).

Figure 7.4   Boat potties like these can work if the sewer system doesn't. Be sure to have enough scented toilet treatment available.

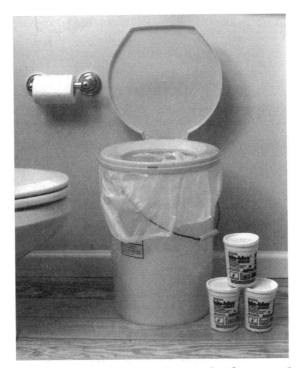

Figure 7.5   Most camping stores sell a toilet seat that fits over a 5-gallon bucket, and you fit a plastic bag into the bucket.

Figure 7.6   Composting toilets need no water or electricity and only have to be emptied once or twice a year after the waste has turned to compost.

Also, there are more expensive composting toilets ($1,000–1,500) that do not use water, chemicals, or electricity that can easily be installed in any house (Figure 7.6). These units are virtually odorless and require a small pipe venting to the outside. The natural heat created by the composting procedure creates a flow out the vent and a downdraft through the seat hole that eliminates odors. You simply empty a tray full of organic compost once or twice a year.[1]

DISPOSAL OF HUMAN WASTE

In any emergency, especially ones that continue for weeks or months, proper disposal of human waste is extremely important. If this is not done properly, diseases such as cholera, hepatitis, amoebic dysentery, etc., can quickly appear and devastate a community.

If you are hooked to a private septic system on your property, just keep flushing your waste down the toilet with waste water, as there is nothing in these systems that will be effected by a disruption. If, however, you are hooked into a central system, and it becomes unusable, you must find an effective way of disposing of all human waste. Local authorities hopefully will notify you quickly with what to do if the sewer plant fails. However, if they do not, you must safely dispose of the waste by effective storage, burning, or burying.

If you are burying human waste, bury it so that animals will not get to it. This means at least 2 feet below ground and well covered. Be sure you are at least 50 feet away from any well, spring, creek, lake, or other water source. You can build a "pit privy" if you need to. You need a hole 3.5 × 3.5 feet and 5 feet deep. Build a 4-foot high wooden riser above it, with a hinged top to keep animals out (and with a hole and a toilet seat in it). Tamp earth around the wooden risers. When the privy fills to within 18 inches of ground level, fill it with dirt (you can add lime as well) and start a new one. Do not build a pit privy on the down slope of a hill. It could leach into the water supply.

HOUSEHOLD GARBAGE

Garbage pickup and disposal may also be interrupted. Even the kitchen sink garbage disposal unit may be useless for awhile. It may be a good time to buy a compost bin (Figure 7.7). These are simple plastic containers that you set out in your yard. You can dump all your organic food waste (except animal products) into the bin and turn it into usable compost for your garden or ornamental plants. Your paper products can be burned, and other waste should be stored in heavy plastic garbage bags until normal garbage pickup and disposal are restored. However, be sure never to put food waste in bags outside, as they can attract anything from rabid dogs to disease-carrying rodents. Also never stack garbage bags near a fire hydrant, which can conceal it from firefighters.

Figure 7.7 Compost bins can be used to turn kitchen waste (except animal products) into usable compost.

Expect delays in garbage collection and other services in emergencies. Rodents can be a major health threat where garbage accumulates, so make sure you have enough sturdy, lidded containers to hold refuse produced over a two-week period. Be prepared to keep your yard clean if other people's refuse finds its way to you.

Don't allow garbage to accumulate outside your home. In some rural areas, trash can be a particular attraction for a variety of wildlife—some dangerous. Store paper and other flammables away from any heat sources or open flames. If waste builds up, consider burying bags in pits, and use lime to cut down on smell and contamination.

WASHING CLOTHES

Washing clothes may become a major issue, especially if any interruption lasts weeks or months. There are small, hand-cranked laundry devices, good for underwear and socks, or even the old nonelectric hand washing machines with hand-cranked wringers[2] (Figure 7.8).

Figure 7.8   Small, hand-cranked washing machines work for small loads. An indoor clothesline can suffice in an emergency.

Figure 7.9   Outdoor clotheslines may blossom during a disaster.

Other than these two options, maybe the best bet is a washboard in your bath tub and an outdoor clothesline (Figure 7.9). If you have a generator, you can probably power your washing machine and, if it's powerful enough, perhaps an electric dryer (or the blower of a gas dryer). You should also look into an indoor clothes line if you do not have one already.

STAYING HEALTHY

Perhaps more than any other area of preparedness, the health and safety issues become quite individualized according to each family's needs. The health needs of each individual must be taken into account to be sure the proper medicines and equipment are available for the duration of any disruption. Also, there is always the threat of food-borne illnesses (see Descriptions, Symptoms, and Preventative Measures at the end of this chapter) from tainted food.

In the past decades there has been huge growth in the home health care field. Many people are now effectively cared for at home who in the past would have required hospital care. Because of this there has also been an increase in medical equipment being used in the home. If anyone in the family uses medical equipment (dialysis machine, IV pump, glucose tester, etc.) consider a small generator to use during outages (Figure 7.10). If there is any nonelectric, non-computerized equipment to replace your existing equipment, it may be wise to have it on hand.

Many of us use some type of prescription drugs. If it's just a pain killer for an occasional ache, we can do without them (Figure 7.11). However, if it's a critical drug, say for high blood pressure, asthma,

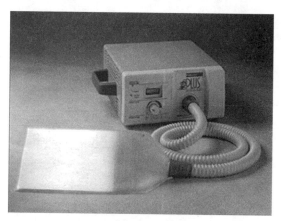

Figure 7.10   Be sure you check with the manufacturers of all medical devices to be sure they will operate properly. Get it in writing.

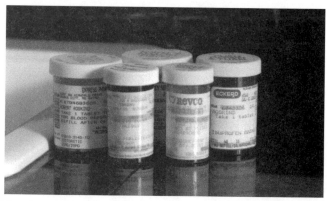

Figure 7.11   Be sure to have adequate stock of needed prescription and off-the-shelf drugs. Your life or health may depend on it.

diabetes, etc., where an interruption can cause health problems, even death, I highly recommend planning for any emergency event with a 2–3 month supply (why gamble with your health or life?). If your doctor will not cooperate, find another one. If your health insurance will not pay for the added months, pay for it yourself. Don't take chances in this area. Pharmaceutical distribution and manufacturing can be disrupted in a major emergency.

Also, you may want to determine if there are any alternative approaches to whatever conditions presently demand that you take prescription drugs. Often herbs, vitamins, relaxation techniques, teas, etc., may help the condition. Talk to your local health food store or get a good book on alternative practices. If any alternative approaches seem feasible to you, lay in a store of the recommended herbs, vitamins, supplements, teas, etc.

In addition to having all the needed prescription medicines, stock a good supply of over-the-counter drugs. Cold medicines, athlete's foot remedies, calamine lotion, cough medicines, antacids, and headache compounds will be much appreciated. Just take a walk through a well-supplied drug department at a discount store and load up.

In addition to the obvious health needs, also consider other, not so obvious health concerns. If any family member has a complex health issue, it may be a good idea to have a copy of their doctor's records in case they need care and your regular doctor is not available. A supply of vitamins and supplements would be a good idea, in case a balanced diet is not so easily obtainable. Also be sure everyone who wears glasses has an extra pair or two.

In addition, emergency health situations may become a major issue. The possibility of fires, accidents, falls, heart attacks, strokes, etc., are greatly increased in these situations. At the same time, the normal 911 emergency response teams and hospital services may be not functioning as efficiently. Indeed, you may be called on to be your own emergency team or doctor.

It would be wise to have at least one person in the household trained in CPR and basic first aid. Also have a good emergency first aid and basic health care book available (a book, not a CD). Get a good first aid kit, not a cheap one from a discount store, or even an expensive one that is made for companies to make available for their employees (these are almost worthless except for minor problems) (Figure 7.12). Get a good-quality first aid kit designed for when a doctor is not available for a long time. Many camping stores or catalogs sell these for $100–150. Even some CPR equipment would not be a bad idea if you want to go to that level of preparedness.

Make sure you and your child's immunizations are up to date, and make sure you have a hard copy of every family members' shot records. The frail, elderly people with particular medical problems requiring a care giver and people with other disabilities must make special plans for their safety in the event that emergency services fail.

Those who have the following conditions may be especially at risk and should take special precautions:

- Acute or chronic respiratory illnesses
- Heart ailments
- Unstable or juvenile diabetes
- Dependence on tube feeding
- Epilepsy
- Tracheotomies

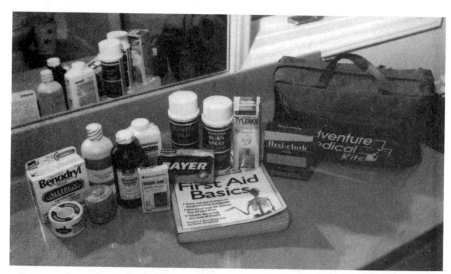

Figure 7.12   Get a good survival first aid kit, not a home first aid kit that assumes medical help is quickly available. Also get a good first aid book and off-the-shelf items.

- Urinary catheters
- Colostomies
- Dialysis dependence

PAPER PRODUCTS

We seldom realize how reliant we are on paper products until they're gone (ever run out of toilet paper on a camping trip?). It would be an excellent idea to store a generous amount of paper products. In stressful times they will make life much easier. If water is in short supply, washing may be wasteful and paper plates, plastic utensils, and cups may be greatly appreciated.

In addition many of the products will reduce the spread of disease and germs, which is a major concern when infrastructures fail. Sponges and cloth cleaning rags can spread disease as they are reused. Paper products that can be discarded after one use may be wiser when conditions degrade. Most Americans give little thought to diseases such as amoebic dysentery and hepatitis that ravage countries with poor sanitation. Remember that our standards of hygiene can revert immediately to those of the Third World if our infrastructure fails, even for a short time.

Have the following products on hand:

- Toilet paper
- Female paper products
- Paper towels
- Napkins
- Facial tissues
- Paper plates
- Paper bowls
- Paper/plastic cups
- Plastic eating utensils (Figure 7.13)

In doing so, it is important to have a storage area for these products. You want all of these products off the ground and away from heat sources. You can store these items with your food storage on storage shelves. Although paper products aren't that heavy, you may

Figure 7.13   Paper products are vital not only for convenience but also to reduce the spread of disease in emergency situations. Have an adequate supply on hand.

wish to store heavier items with them, so make sure you have sturdy shelves. Some storage shelves require lots of assembly and if you assemble them wrong, you may have structural problems. Know what height and width you need. If you have 8-foot ceilings, you may be disappointed with 60-inch shelves.

STAYING SAFE

In addition to staying healthy, you need to consider staying safe, not only from the usual threats in a normally operating world, but from new or increased threats in a disrupted world. A battery-operated or photoelectric smoke detector and carbon monoxide detector are highly recommended, as the ones wired directly into your electrical system may not work if the power goes off unless they have a battery back-

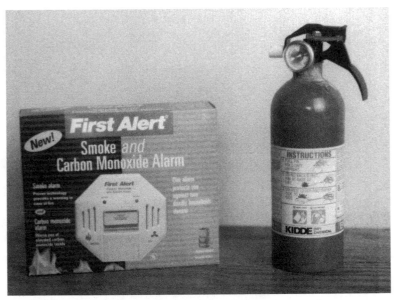

Figure 7.14   Install a battery-operated smoke and carbon monoxide detector and have several fire extinguishers in well-known places.

up. And remember you may be using equipment for lighting, cooking, and heating that increases your fire threat (Figure 7.14).

You will need a complete list of all emergency phone numbers (police, fire, doctor, Red Cross, FEMA, utility companies, etc.) posted where everyone knows where they are. However, if the phones are down, these will not be much use. Be sure that all cars have a full tank of gas and that you have clear instructions how to get to:

▪ Closest hospital
▪ Fire station
▪ Police station
▪ Doctor's office
▪ Gas company
▪ Dentist's office

Be sure you have several fire extinguishers around and test them if they are very old and may have lost their charge. If you rely on a security system, this may be incapacitated, and let's face it, crime may increase if police officers are overloaded and people are in greater need. You may want to add a few locks or deadbolts, steel doors, solar-powered motion detecting devices, floodlights, a battery-operated security system, etc. Also be sure to store any cash (have enough on hand for however long you feel the problems may last), valuables, gold, or important documents in fire-resistant boxes ($20 at any home center), safes, or the safety deposit box at the bank (Figure 7.15).

If electronic locks rely on electricity, it's likely they either won't open, possibly locking a person in or out, or fail in "safe mode" by releasing the lock. Check to see if there is a manual override; if there is, make sure you have the key or information to use it. If not, you may need to force the door if entry or egress is necessary.

If you need to leave your home, it is a good idea to have many of the items in this chapter readily available in smaller sizes in a kit so that you can move quickly if necessary. You may want to have these and other staple bath products ready in a backpack just in case.

Figure 7.15　　Fire-resistant safes and boxes are needed if you are storing valuables, important papers, or cash.

NOTES

[1] Jade Mountain, 800-442-1972, www.jademountain.com (Be sure to mention #241 book.) and The Survival Center, 1-800-321-2900, http://survivalcenter.com
[2] Ibid.

CHECKLIST FOR HEALTH, SAFETY, AND CLEANLINESS
(Compliments of Y2K Women: www.y2kwomen.com)

❑ Bleach
❑ Dish washing detergent (antibacterial)
❑ Dishpan
❑ Drying rack
❑ Dishtowels
❑ Hand soap (antibacterial)
❑ Hand soap (waterless)
❑ Sponges
❑ Steel wool pads (Brillo)
❑ Rubber gloves
❑ Cleanser with bleach
❑ Trash bags
❑ Drawstring, white, tall kitchen bags
❑ Black garbage bags
❑ Twisties
❑ Baggies (zip lock)
❑ Small
❑ Sandwich size
❑ Large
❑ Thick, freezer bags
❑ Aluminum foil (various sizes)
❑ Plastic wrap
❑ Paper towels
❑ Paper napkins
❑ Rags
❑ Water filters

- ❏ Water purifiers
- ❏ Iodine
- ❏ Manual can opener
- ❏ Knife sharpener
- ❏ Kitchen matches (in waterproof container)
- ❏ Fire extinguisher
- ❏ _____
- ❏ _____
- ❏ Detergent (liquid laundry soap)
- ❏ Bleach
- ❏ Drying rack
- ❏ Clothes line
- ❏ Clothes pins
- ❏ Washtub
- ❏ Buckets
- ❏ Furniture polish
- ❏ Window cleaner
- ❏ Dust cloths
- ❏ Disinfectant (Lysol)
- ❏ Broom
- ❏ Air freshener
- ❏ Toilet bowl cleaner
- ❏ Plunger
- ❏ Drain snake
- ❏ Drain unclogger (like Drano)
- ❏ Sewing kit
- ❏ Needles
- ❏ Thread
- ❏ Scissors
- ❏ Material

SHOWER AND TUB

- ❏ Bubble bath (!)
- ❏ Bath soap
- ❏ Outdoor solar shower bag
- ❏ Razor and blades
- ❏ Shampoo/conditioner

❑   Shaving cream
❑   Tissues
❑   Toilet paper
❑   Moist towelettes or baby wipes
❑   Air freshener
❑   _____
❑   _____

FEMININE HYGIENE

❑   Maxi Pads
❑   Tampons
❑   Panty liners
❑   Menstrual cup (the keeper)
❑   Washable pads
❑   _____
❑   _____

HAIR CARE

❑   Hair brushes
❑   Combs
❑   Elastics and ribbons for little girls
❑   Nonelectric curlers (like the little velcro kind)
❑   Curling iron (propane)
❑   Hair cutting scissors
❑   _____
❑   _____

DENTAL CARE

❑   Toothbrushes
❑   Toothpaste
❑   Mouthwash
❑   Dental floss
❑   Denture care products
❑   Adhesive
❑   Cleanser

EYE CARE

- ❑ Extra glasses
- ❑ Extra replacement screws
- ❑ Extra contacts
- ❑ Saline solution
- ❑ _____

MAKEUP

Don't discount this as unimportant! If wearing makeup is part of your lifestyle, make sure that you include enough to last you for awhile. It's important to feel good about how you look! It helps your self-esteem which will help your family.

- ❑ Cleanser
- ❑ Toner
- ❑ Moisturizer
- ❑ Foundation
- ❑ Blush
- ❑ Eyeliner
- ❑ Eye shadow
- ❑ Mascara
- ❑ _____
- ❑ _____

PERSONAL GROOMING

- ❑ Deodorant
- ❑ Perfume
- ❑ Hair spray
- ❑ Hair color (Ladies, stock up on the L'oreal now!)
- ❑ Permanent wave solution (curlers and papers)
- ❑ Hair relaxer

Checklist Medicine Cabinet

NONPRESCRIPTION MEDICATIONS

- ❑ Activated charcoal (use if indicated for certain poisons)
- ❑ Advil (Ibuprofen)
- ❑ Aleve
- ❑ Antacid (for stomach upset)
- ❑ Antidiarrhea medication (Kaopectate; Pepto-Bismol)
- ❑ Aspirin
- ❑ Benadryl
- ❑ Cold, flu, and cough remedies
- ❑ Cough drops
- ❑ Nyquil/Dayquil
- ❑ Hay fever/sinus
- ❑ Hydrocortisone creme (Cortaid)
- ❑ Laxatives for constipation
- ❑ Motrin
- ❑ Neosporin
- ❑ Syrup of Ipecac (use to induce vomiting)
- ❑ Tylenol (Acetaminophen)
- ❑ Yeast infection medicine
- ❑ _____
- ❑ _____

MEDICAL CONCERNS FOR YOUNG CHILDREN

- ❑ Band-Aids in lots of sizes
- ❑ Children's Tylenol
- ❑ Diaper rash cream
- ❑ Digital thermometer for young babies
- ❑ Ear viewer and instructions
- ❑ Immunization Records
- ❑ Pedialyte (electrolyte fluid)
- ❑ Specific medicines for your child (check on the shelf life of medications)
- ❑ _____
- ❑ _____

ALTERNATIVE AND NATURAL HEALTH

Note: Although herbal remedies are nonprescription, they can still be dangerous if used improperly. Please read all labels for directions and keep out of the reach of children.

- ❑ Echinacea with Goldenseal for colds
- ❑ Cool Cayenne for upper respiratory
- ❑ L-Lysine for canker sores
- ❑ Aloe for burns
- ❑ Melatonin for insomnia
- ❑ Zinc lozenges for sore throats
- ❑ _____
- ❑ _____

MEDICAL SUPPLIES

- ❑ Ammonia
- ❑ Glucose
- ❑ Hydrogen peroxide
- ❑ Insect bite/sting topical medicine
- ❑ Insect repellent
- ❑ Iodine
- ❑ Petroleum jelly
- ❑ Rubbing alcohol
- ❑ _____
- ❑ _____

FEMININE

- ❑ Hormone replacement medications
- ❑ Yeast infection medication
- ❑ Wild yam cream
- ❑ Tampons/sanitary pads

FIRST AID KIT (RECOMMENDED FEMA LIST)

Assemble a first aid kit for your home and one for each car. A first aid kit* should include:

- ❑ Sterile adhesive bandages in assorted sizes
- ❑ 2-inch sterile gauze pads (4-6)
- ❑ 4-inch sterile gauze pads (4-6)
- ❑ Hypoallergenic adhesive tape
- ❑ Triangular bandages (3)
- ❑ 2-inch sterile roller bandages (3 rolls)
- ❑ 3-inch sterile roller bandages (3 rolls)
- ❑ Scissors
- ❑ Tweezers
- ❑ Needle
- ❑ Moistened towelettes
- ❑ Antiseptic
- ❑ Thermometer
- ❑ Tongue blades (2)
- ❑ Tube of petroleum jelly or other lubricant
- ❑ Cleansing agent/soap
- ❑ Latex gloves (2 pair)
- ❑ Sunscreen

*Contact your local American Red Cross chapter to obtain a basic first aid manual.

NONPRESCRIPTION DRUGS

- ❑ Aspirin or non-aspirin pain reliever
- ❑ Antidiarrhea medication
- ❑ Antacid (for stomach upset)
- ❑ Syrup of Ipecac (use to induce vomiting)
- ❑ Laxative
- ❑ Activated charcoal
- ❑ Cold medicine/cough syrup
- ❑ _____
- ❑ _____

Tools and Supplies (Recommended FEMA list)

❑ Mess kits, or paper cups, plates, and plastic utensils
❑ Emergency preparedness manual
❑ Battery-operated radio and extra batteries
❑ Flashlight and extra batteries
❑ Cash or traveler's checks, change
❑ Nonelectric can opener, utility knife
❑ Fire extinguisher: small canister, ABC type
❑ Tube tent
❑ Pliers
❑ Tape
❑ Compass
❑ Matches in a waterproof container
❑ Aluminum foil
❑ Plastic storage containers
❑ Signal flare
❑ Paper, pencil
❑ Needles, thread
❑ Medicine dropper
❑ Shut-off wrench to turn off household gas and water
❑ Whistle
❑ Plastic sheeting
❑ Map of the area (for locating shelters)

Clothing and Bedding*

❑ Sturdy shoes or work boots
❑ Hat and gloves
❑ Rain gear
❑ Thermal underwear
❑ Blankets or sleeping bags
❑ Sunglasses
❑ _____

* Include at least one complete change of clothing and footwear per person.

FOR BABY

- ❏ Formula
- ❏ Diapers
- ❏ Bottles
- ❏ Powdered milk
- ❏ Medications
- ❏ Wipes

FOR ADULTS

- ❏ Heart and high blood pressure medication
- ❏ Insulin
- ❏ Prescription drugs
- ❏ Denture needs
- ❏ Contact lenses and supplies
- ❏ Extra eye glasses

CREATE A FAMILY DISASTER PLAN (RECOMMENDED FEMA LIST)

To get started:

- Contact your local emergency management or civil defense office and your local American Red Cross chapter.
- Find out which disasters are most likely to happen in your community.
- Ask how you would be warned.
- Find out how to prepare for each.
- Meet with your family.
- Discuss the types of disasters that could occur.
- Explain how to prepare and respond.
- Discuss what to do if advised to evacuate.
- Practice what you have discussed.
- Plan how your family will stay in contact if separated by disaster.
- Pick two meeting places:
  1. A location a safe distance from your home in case of fire.
  2. A place outside your neighborhood in case you can't return home.

- Choose an out-of-state friend as a "check-in contact" for everyone to call.
- Complete these steps:
  1. Post emergency telephone numbers by every phone.
  2. Show responsible family members how and when to shut off water, gas, and electricity at main switches.
  3. Install a smoke detector (battery operated) on each level of your home, especially near bedrooms; test monthly and change the batteries two times each year.
  4. Contact your local fire department to learn about home fire hazards.
  5. Learn first aid and CPR. Contact your local American Red Cross chapter for information and training.
- Meet with your neighbors.
- Plan how the neighborhood could work together after a disaster. Know your neighbors' skills (medical, technical). Consider how you could help neighbors who have special needs, such as elderly or disabled persons.
- Make plans for child care in case parents can't get home.
- Remember to practice and maintain your plan.

The Federal Emergency Management Agency's Community and Family Preparedness Program and the American Red Cross Disaster Education Program are nationwide efforts to help people prepare for disasters of all types. For more information, please contact your local or state office of Emergency Management, and your local American Red Cross chapter. Ask for "Your Family Disaster Plan" and the "Emergency Preparedness Checklist." Or write to FEMA, P.O. Box 70274 Washington, DC 20024 FEMA L, 189 ARC 4463.

RED CROSS EMERGENCY HANDBOOK

How to Cope With...

- Accidents, Injuries, and Sudden Illness
- Choking
- Fire, Flood, and Earthquake
- Water Rescue
- Family Problems Caused by Military Service

Emergency Telephone Numbers:

Fire _____

Police _____

Doctor_____

Ambulance _____

Poison Control _____

Red Cross _____

....
Wounds

Control bleeding.

   a. Apply direct pressure on wound with a sterile dressing (if available).

   b. Elevate injured area above the heart if possible.

   c. Apply pressure to supplying blood vessel if direct pressure is not successful.

Secure dry, sterile dressings with bandages.

Cleanse minor injuries thoroughly with plain soap and water (clean your hands first).

If evidence of infection appears, see a doctor.

Fractures

Do not move the victim.

Keep the broken bone ends and adjacent joints from moving.

If an open wound is present, control the bleeding (see wounds).

Apply splints.

Shock

Keep victim lying down.

Cover him only enough to keep him from losing body heat.

Obtain medical help as soon as possible.

In Case of a Serious Accident

RESCUE: Do not move victim unless further danger is imminent.

CHECK BREATHING: If not breathing, give artificial respiration.

CONTROL SEVERE BLEEDING: Use direct pressure and elevate.

DILUTE POISONS: With milk or water.

TREAT FOR SHOCK

CALL FOR HELP

GIVE THIS INFORMATION:

    L—Location of emergency (address and phone number)
    I—Injury (number and type)
    F—First aid given
    E—Equipment needed or available

....
Poisoning

Dilute with milk or water (except for an unconscious person).

Call poison information center.

If breathing stops, use artificial respiration (see below).

Save label of poison container and/or save sample of vomit if victim regurgitates.

Transport to hospital emergency room.

....
Burns

To relieve pain and prevent contamination:

   a. Submerge small minor burns in cold water (do not use ice).

   b. Apply sterile dressings to large extensive burns (do not apply grease or ointment).

Treat for shock.

Seek medical assistance.

....
Stoppage of Breathing

Give artificial respiration—Mouth to mouth method.

   a. Tip victim's head back, chin pointing up.

   b. Look, listen and feel for breathing.

   c. If not breathing, close victim's nostrils by pinching shut.

   d. Make a tight seal over victim's mouth with your mouth.

   e. Inflate victim's lungs with 2 full slow breaths.

   f. Watch victim's chest fall while listening for air return between breaths.

   g. Check for the pulse at the side of the neck for 5 seconds. If there is no pulse and there is no breathing, begin CPR if you have been trained.

   h. If victim has a pulse, but is not breathing, give artificial respiration.

   i. Breathe for adults once every 5 seconds; for children, once every 4 seconds; for infants, once every 3 seconds.

   j. Recheck for spontaneous breathing every few minutes

Call an ambulance.

....
Heart Attack

SYMPTOMS:

Chest pains, difficulty breathing, nausea, sweating, weak rapid pulse. If you suspect a person has suffered a heart attack, search for an identification card or bracelet for additional steps or doctor's telephone number. Question eye witnesses about what has occurred.

FIRST AID:

Place the victim in a comfortable position.

Raise his head and chest if breathing is difficult.

If breathing stops, apply artificial respiration.

Get medical aid fast—physician or person trained in CPR.

If pulse becomes absent, give CPR if trained.

   a. Tip head to open airway. Look, listen, feel for breathing.
   b. Restore breathing. Give mouth-to-mouth artificial respiration.
   c. Restore circulation. Check carotid pulse. If absent, apply external cardiac compression on the victim's breast bone.

Single Rescuer: 15 chest compressions at 80–100 per minute, alternate with 2 slow full lung inflations, then repeat 15 compressions.

Two Rescuers: 5 compressions at 90–100 per minute. Give 1 breath every 5th compression. Repeat at 5:1 ratio.

....
Simple Fainting

Keep victim lying down with feet elevated until recovery is complete.

Bathe face down gently with cool water. Do not pour water over victim.

Loosen tight clothing. Keep crowds away.

....
Heat Exhaustion

Provide rest, with feet elevated 8–12 inches.

Apply cool, wet cloths or rubbing alcohol to the victim.

Give sips of cool water, ½ glass every 15 minutes for 1 hour.

Loosen clothing.

Fan victim.

Victim should do no work for several days.

....
Frostbite

Protect the frozen area from further injury.

Cover the frozen area with clothing or blankets.

Do not rub frozen part since this may cause tissue death.

Immerse chilled part in warm water (102–108°) as soon as possible.

If thawed and refrozen, immerse chilled part in room temperature water (70–74°).

Do not use heat lamp, hot water bottle, or stove to warm the frostbitten area.

Discontinue warming the victim as soon as the affected part becomes flush.

If fingers or toes are involved, place dry sterile gauze between them to keep them separated.

If medical help is not available for 1 hour or more, give victim (conscious victims only) a weak solution of salt and soda at home or en route: 1 level teaspoon of salt and 1/2 level teaspoon of baking soda to each quart of water, neither hot or cold. Give about 4 ounces of 1/2 glass every 15 minutes (adults).

Take a Red Cross course.

....
Water Rescue

You can help...even if you can't swim.

When a bather is in trouble near a dock, float, or side of pool, your number one priority is to stay on the dock.

Extend upper body over water, making sure you have a firm foothold.

- Grasp victim's wrists.
- Slowly draw victim to safety.

Or...

- Extend a pole, towel, shirt, or branch to victim.
- Draw victim to safety—don't let victim pull you into water!

Or...

- Use buoy or other flotation device attached to rope. Stand on one end of rope, throw float beyond victim and slowly pull it into victim's grasp. In a boat, on a beach, in shallow water... think first. Use oar, paddle, or a piece of wood.

Don't...

- Let the victim pull you in over your head, or there may be two victims.
- Attempt a swimming rescue unless you are a trained lifesaver.

Home Safety Tips

- Keep stove and sink areas well lighted.
- Turn pot handles away from front of stove but not over another burner.
- Wipe up spilled grease or fluids immediately.
- Cut away from you when using a knife, and keep knives in rack or drawer compartment.
- Dry hands before using electrical appliances and never use such appliances while in the bathtub.
- Use a step stool to reach high cupboards.
- Have cracked or frayed electrical cords replaced by a qualified electrician.
- Avoid wearing loose clothing around fire and don't use hair sprays near a flame or while smoking.

- Screen fireplaces.
- Use large, deep ashtrays and never smoke in bed or when you're likely to doze off.
- Keep insecticides, disinfectants, household cleaners, and medicines in original, clearly labeled containers and out of reach of children.
- Keep list of emergency telephone numbers—doctor, police, fire, utilities, ambulance service, rescue squad, poison control center—near telephone.
- Keep walking areas and door entries clear of obstructions and tripping hazards. Have non-skid backing on small rugs and keep such rugs away from heads of stairs.
- Keep heavy traffic areas well lighted.
- Avoid carrying loads that block your vision.
- Keep stairs clear of toys and other stumbling blocks, and keep them well lighted at top and bottom. Keep treads and carpeting in good repair.
- Have sturdy handrails, indoors and on porches, and sturdy banisters on open stairs and stairwells.
- Equip tubs and showers with nonskid mats or textured surfaces and sturdy handbars, and keep nonskid bath rugs in front of tubs and showers.
- Keep night lights in bathrooms for elderly persons and children.
- Clean up floor spills and debris quickly.

FOOD-BORNE ILLNESSES
(From How-To Survival Library:www.y2klibrary.com)

Name of illness	What causes it	Symptoms	Characteristics of illness	Preventative measures
Salmonellosis Examples of foods involved: poultry, red meats, eggs, dried foods, and dairy products.	*Salmonellae.* This bacteria is wide-spread in nature and lives and grows in the intestinal tracts of human beings and animals.	Sever headache, followed by vomiting, diarrhea, abdominal cramps, and fever. Infants, elderly, and persons with low resistance are most susceptible. Sever infections cause high fever and may even cause death.	Transmitted by eating contaminated food, or by contact with infected persons or carriers of the infection. Also transmitted by insects, rodents, and pets. Onset: Usually within 12 to 36 hours. Duration: 2–7 days.	Salmonellae in food are destroyed by heating the food to 140°F and holding for 10 minutes or to higher temperatures for less time; for instance, 155°F for a few seconds. Refrigeration at 40°F inhibits the increase of Salmonellae, but they remain alive in foods in the refrigerator or freezer, and even in dried foods.
Perfringens Examples of foods involved: stews, soups, or gravies made from poultry or red meat.	*Clostridium Perfringens.* Spore-forming bacteria that grow in the absence of oxygen. Temperatures reached in thorough cooking of most foods are sufficient to destroy vegetative cells, but heat-resistant spores can survive.	Nausea without vomiting, diarrhea, acute inflammation of stomach and intestines.	Transmitted by eating food contaminated with abnormally large numbers of the bacteria. Onset: Usually within 8 to 20 hours. Duration: May persist for 24 hours.	To prevent growth of surviving bacteria in cooked meats, gravies, and meat casseroles that are to be eaten later, cool foods rapidly and refrigerate promptly at 40°F or below, or hold them about 140°F.

Name of illness	What causes it	Symptoms	Characteristics of illness	Preventative measures
Staphylococcal poisoning (frequently called staph) Examples of foods involved: custards, egg salad, potato salad, chicken salad, macaroni salad, ham, salami, and cheese.	*Staphylococcus aureus*. Bacteria fairly resistant to heat. Bacteria growing in food produce a toxin that is extremely resistant to heat.	Vomiting, diarrhea, prostration, abdominal cramps. Generally mild and often attributed to other causes.	Transmitted by food handlers who carry the bacteria and by eating food containing the toxin.	Growth of bacteria that produces toxin is inhibited by keeping hot foods above 140°F and cold foods at or below 40°F. Toxin is destroyed by boiling for several hours, or heating the food in a pressure cooker at 240°F for 30 minutes.
Botulism Examples of foods involved: canned low-acid foods, and smoked fish	*Clostridium botulinum*. Spore-forming organisms that grow and produce toxin in the absence of oxygen, such as in a sealed container.	Double vision, inability to swallow, speech difficulty, progressive respiratory paralysis. Fatality rate is high, about 65% in the United States.	Transmitted by eating food containing the toxin. Onset: Usually within 12 to 36 hours or longer. Duration: 3 to 6 days.	Bacterial spores in food are destroyed by high temperatures obtained only in the pressure canner. More than 6 hours is needed to kill the spores at boiling temperature (212°F). The toxin is destroyed by boiling for 10 to 20 minutes; time required depends on kind of food.

COMMUNICATIONS AND IMPORTANT PAPERS

"Y2K offers an opportunity for individual and collective psychospiritual growth. We get pushed to our limits and then some, over and over, in endlessly new ways. We are (and will be) continually presented with intense choices: to grow very big or shrink very small, to break through or break down, to let go or be torn apart. The positive direction is often quite clear but exceedingly difficult. And sometimes it is unclear, and we must decide anyway. If we rise to the occasion, we will often (but not always) suddenly find ourselves larger, suddenly more able to make space for those who couldn't or wouldn't take the harder path, those who are struggling or suffering. Other times it may just feel like we are being broken down. It is a time of testing."
— Tom Atlee of The Co-Intelligence Institute

COMMUNICATION

The Problem

There is a distinct possibility that the normal communication systems (phone, Internet, telegraph, postal delivery, FedEx, UPS, etc.) may experience disruptions in many disasters. In addition, if you rely on the phone, TV, and radios for your contact with emergency services, there is the possibility you may be unable to get information if you are not prepared. The Internet may also be at risk. If you rely on this for your business or personal needs, it would be wise to make alternative plans.

The Solution

One-way communications, bulletins from emergency services, FEMA, Red Cross, etc., are usually easy to maintain with a battery operated radio or TV. Two-way communications, such as phone, e-mail, etc., may be impossible until services are restored. There is little you can do to assure phone service, other than hope the telephone companies, large and small, fix it in time (Figure 8.1). You may want to consider

Figure 8.1   Hopefully both your local service provider and long-distance provider will be ready in time.

Figure 8.2   Cell phones may work when other phones don't—and vice versa.

having a cellular phone as well as conventional service. The cellular system may work when the conventional system does not, and vice versa. If you get a cell phone, it may be best to get service from a large provider (Figure 8.2).

Getting news from the outside world after the power goes off is as easy as using a battery-powered radio or TV. You can even get radios that you wind up for 3 minutes and then play for 30 minutes, or solar-powered units so you never need batteries. However, a small radio can go a very long time on one set of batteries. You may want to get a radio that also offers shortwave so that you can pick up news from other states and countries.

Short of carrier pigeons, almost all forms of two-way communication are very expensive to supply on your own. If electrical power is down in your area, but your phone company has alternative power or is in an area where electricity is working, your phone may still work if you have a phone that doesn't require an external AC power supply. Many cordless phones don't work if the power is out. Also, some of the integrated phone/answering machine devices need power. If your phone plugs into a 110-V electric socket in addition to the phone jack, check and see if it works when unplugged from the electrical socket. If not, go buy a cheap phone that works on just the phone jack alone without the need of external power supply. This way you might be able to use your phone in an electrical outage.

The option to the average homeowner to be able to effectively communicate with others should these systems fail are few and expensive. They include handheld walkie talkies, CB radios, ham radios, shortwave radios, and short-range telemobile and satellite telephone systems. All of these systems have severe drawbacks in regard to how many people can be contacted, how far they reach, and how much they cost. Because of this, most of us will just stay *incommunicado* until normal systems are restored.

HANDHELD WALKIE TALKIE

There is a new generation of battery-operated handheld walkie talkies available at most electronic stores or large discount stores. Though they claim ranges of a mile, this depends greatly on the terrain. Any hills or trees greatly reduce their range. They cost around $100 per unit and require batteries (which must be replaced often). Marine VHF radios are good for 50–100 miles. This VHF are only to be used by boats and ships but in emergency they could be used on land.

CB RADIOS

CB (Citizens Band) radios have been around for years and are used so that a base (i.e., a dispatcher) can talk to many subunits (i.e., company trucks). It also allows the subunits to all talk to each other. These units cost approximately $40–200 each and can be used either with AC or batteries (any car battery will work). Their range is between 1 and 10 miles (longer if conditions are right). The reason for this broad range is that conditions such as terrain, weather, sunspots, etc., will all make a difference. This may be a viable option if you want to remain in constant contact with friends or loved ones in your immediate area.

HAM RADIOS

Across the world there is a system of ham radios (or amateur radios), a noncommercial system of personal communication. There are over two million ham operators in the world, with over 600,000 in the United States. There is no age restriction for operators, and though this is mostly a hobby, in emergencies ham operators are of great value. Though the range varies, by subscribing to a local repeater service, ham radio operators are able to talk with other ham operators all over the world (something to consider in a worldwide emergency). They cost around $200 and require an operator's license (easily obtainable with a little study of the rules and regulations).

Ham radio equipment can operate on electricity, batteries, or solar units. With batteries and portable solar units, the transmitters and receivers can be carried from place to place, so that ham operators can be "stationed" in various locales during an emergency. Handheld devices are also available. For more information on amateur radio see Beginner's Guide to Ham Radio, online at http://www.irony.com/ham-howto.html

Or contact Amateur Radio, Relay League, Colorado Public Information Coordinator, Erik Dyce, (303) 751-4605.

PORTABLE SATELLITE PHONE SYSTEMS

Though there are private satellite phones that will allow you to talk to another person who has the same system, these are very expensive ($3,000–5,000, plus $1.50 per minute) and still rely on a satellite operating correctly. If you can afford it and staying in touch with a few people is vital or important to you, this may be an option. They can be battery operated, are the size of a briefcase, and include their own small antennae.[1]

IMPORTANT PAPERS

It would be a good idea to have copies of important papers in case you need them and access to them is interrupted. If you keep these papers in a safe-deposit box, you may want to have copies at home (in a fireproof security box) for any papers that they may be needed after a disaster. It is especially important to make sure you have your bank statements, your 401K, IRA, retirement account, stock, bond, and other financial instruments and insurance policy records. Any proof of ownership, whether it be your car, or your boat, or your house, should also be available to you. Also you may want to have several hundred dollars in cash available, in case normal ATMs and banks are out.

If you find that you have to leave your residence for whatever reason, you may want to be able to take all or part of your documentation with you. So be prepared to be able to pick it up and run. Have it well organized and totally up-to-date.

Also, be sure you have duplicates of any medical or dental records that may be needed and not available through the normal channels. Birth certificates, marriage records, passports, citizenship papers, deeds, car registration, promissory notes, and other important papers should be kept at home in a fireproof box ($20 at any home center) in case you cannot access your safe deposit box or normal records.

Important Papers to Have Available

Birth certificates for each member of your family
Marriage licenses or certificates
Baptismal, confirmation, ordination, and other religious records
Social Security cards and financial information
Deeds, titles, car titles, and other proofs of ownership
Mortgages and other loan agreements
Passports
Citizenship papers
Promissory notes
Wills
Power of attorney
Living wills
Loan statements showing exactly what you owe
Credit card statements
Insurance policies and proof of premium payment
Tax returns
Membership papers
Contracts and other legal documents
Diplomas and academic transcripts
Medical, dental, and pharmaceutical records
Bank statements
401K, IRA, retirement account
Stock, bond, and other financial instruments

NOTE

[1] Jade Mountain, 1-800-442-1972, www.jademountain.com (Be sure to mention #241) and The Survival Center, 1-800-321-2900, http://survivalcenter.com

CHILDREN & PETS

"Adults must cope with their own natural feelings of helplessness, fear, and anger before helping children."
—FEMA (Federal Emergency Management Agency)

CHILDREN & DISASTERS

Preparing for disasters, and recovering after one, needs added consideration if children are involved. We must consider their physical needs in preparing for possible disasters. However, as importantly, we must consider their emotional needs after any disaster. Children, more so than adults, can be traumatized emotionally by disasters.

Preparing Children Before a Disaster
WHAT TO STORE

As you prepare your home for any potential disaster or loss of infrastructure, take your children's specific needs into account. Many children become nauseous when scared, so be sure you have foods that can be eaten on an upset stomach. Emergency food bars, fruit rolls, dried fruits, raisins, etc. are nutritious, tasty, and easily digestible on an upset stomach. Spam or canned tuna is not. Store some "comfort foods" (candy, gum, cookies, chips, etc.). Emergencies are not the time to fight over eating habits.

As you store various survival items, also consider the following for children:

- Games, toys, and sports equipment to keep them occupied
- Children's books (pleasant ones—not scary ones)
- Art supplies
- Children's favorite foods
- Children's vitamins
- Extra water (active children may require 1.5-2 gallons per day
- Children's prescription and non-prescription medicines (especially children's anti-acids, headache relief, and diarrhea)
- Extra underwear in case of accidents or diarrhea
- 12-hour light sticks
- Extra glasses
- Family pictures
- Space blankets
- Discarded, but loved, old toys, blankets, or stuffed animals

HOW TO PREPARE CHILDREN FOR POSSIBLE DISASTERS:

In a calm manner, explain to your children about the possibility of any possible disaster. You want to send two distinct messages to them in this conversation: that what you are telling them is very important and that everything will be OK in the end. If you seem fearful, they will become fearful, and remember, kids can grow fears way beyond reason.

The main fears of children in a disaster are:

- Fear of separation
- Fear of the dark
- Fear of abandonment
- Fear of death
- Fear of animals

Talk to your children about possible disasters. Let your child know that life will return to normal after a disaster hits and that many people have gone through these disasters. Reassure them that you will find them if you are not together should a disaster happen. Children's fears are intensified when adults refuse or are reluctant to discuss them with children. They may be told of possible disaster in the school yard or classroom, and if parents will not discuss it with them it can be unsettling. Don't tell them, "It probably won't ever happen, so don't worry your pretty little head about it." Take the time to talk with them.

Every family should have a "Family Disaster Plan" (See "Family Disaster Plan" in reference section). Then meet with the entire family and explain the plan to them. Be sure to:

- Post emergency phone numbers
- Post family and friends' phone numbers
- Select and post out-of-state contact numbers
- Assemble portable disaster kits
- Do an emergency drill

Teach your children how to recognize the warning signs of any disasters that might occur in your area and what to do to protect themselves. Be sure they know what smoke detectors, fire alarms, and warning sirens sound like. Be sure they understand how, and when, to use 911 and to call for help. If they are old enough, have them memorize key contact phone numbers. Be sure they clearly understand what they should do if a disaster hits and you are not with them. At school, the teachers will take charge. However, if they are at a friend's house, at a store or mall, or roaming the neighborhood they must know what to do. A child's first reaction if they are scared is to run home. This may not be wise if a tornado is quickly approaching. Be sure they have a "special meeting place" to go to after the disaster if they are not with an adult.

AFTER A DISASTER:

Remember that after a disaster children's fears may be greatly intensified, even after everything returns to normal. If we do not actively assist them in these fears they can remain for a lifetime. Encourage them to talk about their fears and express them through art or play. Handle them with understanding and kindness.

FOLLOWING A DISASTER SOME CHILDREN MAY[1]:

- Be upset at the loss of a favorite toy, blanket, teddy bear, etc.
- Hit, throw, kick to show their anger.
- Become more active and restless.
- Be afraid of the disaster recurring.
- Ask many times, "Will it come again?"
- Be afraid to be left alone or afraid to sleep alone. Children may want to sleep with a parent or another person.
- Have nightmares.
- Behave as they did when younger. They may start sucking their thumb, wetting the bed, asking for a bottle, wanting to be held.
- Have symptoms of illness such as nausea, vomiting, headaches, not wanting to eat, running a fever.
- Be quiet and withdrawn, not wanting to talk about the experience. Become upset easily—crying and whining frequently.
- Feel guilty that they caused the disaster because of some previous behavior.
- Feel neglected by parents who are busy trying to clean up and rebuild their lives and homes.
- Refuse to go to school or to child care arrangements. The child may not want to be out of the parent's sight.
- Become afraid of loud noises, rain, storms.
- Not show any outward sign of being upset.

Some children may never show distress because they do not feel upset. Other children may not give evidence of being upset until several weeks or months later.

WHAT PARENTS CAN DO TO HELP CHILDREN COPE WITH FEELINGS[2]:

- Talk with your child, providing simple, accurate information to questions.
- Talk with your child about your own feelings.
- Listen to what your child says and how your child says it. Is there fear, anxiety, insecurity? Repeating the child's words may be very helpful, such as "You are afraid that...", or "You wonder

if the storm will come again tonight." This helps both you and the child clarify feelings.

- Reassure your child, "We are together. We care about you. We will take care of you."
- You may need to repeat information and reassurances many times. Do not stop responding just because you told the child once or even 10 times.
- Hold your child. Provide comfort. Touching is important for children during this period. Close contact helps assure children that you are there and will not abandon them.
- Spend extra time putting your child to bed. Talk and offer assurance.
- Leave a night light on if that makes the child feel more secure.
- Observe your child at play. Listen to what is said and how the child plays. Frequently children express feelings of fear or anger while playing with dolls, trucks, or friends after a major disaster.
- Provide play experiences to relieve tension. Work with play-dough, paint, play in water, etc. If children show a need to hit or kick, give them something safe like a pillow, ball, or balloon.
- Allow a safe, open space for them to play if possible.
- If your child lost a meaningful toy or blanket, allow the child to mourn and grieve (by crying, perhaps). It is all part of helping the young child cope with feelings about the disaster. In time, it may be helpful to replace the lost object.
- If you need help for your child, contact family members, grandparents, or a clergy member.

Children and Their Response to Disaster[3]

Children depend on daily routines: They wake up, eat breakfast, go to school, play with friends. When emergencies or disasters interrupt this routine, children may become anxious.

In a disaster, they'll look to you and other adults for help. How you react to an emergency gives them clues on how to act. If you react with alarm, a child may become more scared. They see our fear as proof that the danger is real. If you seem overcome with a sense of loss, a child may feel their losses more strongly.

Children's fears also may stem from their imagination, and you should take these feelings seriously. A child who feels afraid is afraid. Your words and actions can provide reassurance. When talking with your child, be sure to present a realistic picture that is both honest and manageable. Feelings of fear are healthy and natural for adults and children. But as an adult, you need to keep control of the situation. When you're sure that danger has passed, concentrate on your child's emotional needs by asking the child what's uppermost in his or her mind.

Having children participate in the family's recovery activities will help them feel that their life will return to "normal." Your response during this time may have a lasting impact. Be aware that after a disaster, children are most afraid that:

- The event will happen again.
- Someone will be injured or killed.
- They will be separated from the family.
- They will be left alone.

Keep the family together. While you look for housing and assistance, you may want to leave your children with relatives or friends. Instead, keep the family together as much as possible and make children a part of what you are doing to get the family back on its feet. Children get anxious, and they'll worry that their parents won't return.

Calmly and firmly explain the situation. As best as you can, tell children what you know about the disaster. Explain what will happen next. For example, say, "Tonight, we will all stay together in the shelter." Get down to the child's eye level and talk to him or her. Encourage children to talk. Let children talk about the disaster and ask questions as much as they want. Encourage children to describe what they're feeling. Listen to what they say. If possible, include the entire family in the discussion.

Include children in recovery activities. Give children chores that are their responsibility. This will help children feel they are part of the recovery. Having a task will help them understand that everything will be all right. You can help children cope by understanding what causes their anxieties and fears. Reassure them with firmness and love. Your children will realize that life will eventually return to normal. If a child does not respond to the above suggestions, seek help from a mental health specialist or a member of the clergy.

PETS & DISASTERS

Pets too must be considered in any disaster planning. Pets can become quite problematic in a disaster or potential disaster. They are seldom allowed at shelters and tend to run away when frightened. Even though they may not be allowed to go to shelters, leaving them behind is also very dangerous and upsetting for both pets and their owners. Leaving pets behind in a disaster is never recommended unless the danger necessitates your fleeing immediately. Proper preparation can offer you more options in providing safety for your pets.

1. Arrange beforehand for a safe shelter. See if hotels or motels in areas you are likely to flee to allow pets or are their animal shelters or vets in their area that do. Ask hotels if the no pet policy would be wavered in emergencies.

2. Ask friends and relatives outside the disaster area if they could care for your pets (and maybe you as well).

3. Call to see if your local vets or animal shelters can care for them or know of recommended places who can.

4. Assemble a portable pet disaster kit. Keep this kit easily accessible and in an easily portable container. The kit should include:

   • Medications and medical records (stored in a waterproof container)

   • A first aid kit

   • Sturdy leashes, harnesses, and/or carriers

   • Current photos of your pets

   • Food, potable water, bowls, cat litter/pan, and can opener

   • Information on feeding schedules, medical conditions, behavior problems

   • The name and number of your veterinarian

   • Pet beds and toys, if easily transportable.

As soon as you are warned about a potential disaster, locate all your pets and bring them home being sure they cannot escape. Be sure they are wearing collars and tags with updated information. You may want to attach the phone number of a friend or relative living outside the disaster zone in case they are lost and you cannot be reached. Also talk to your neighbors about helping out if you are not at home when the disaster warning occurs. Be sure to keep your pets well leashed as even the best-trained pets can bolt in disasters. Put cats in a carrier.

Birds should be placed in a secure cage. Wrap the cage in a blanket if the weather is cold. Place some fresh fruit in the cage so they will have both food and moisture. Snakes can be put in pillowcases and then transferred to more secure housing when you reach shelter. Bring food, a large water bowl and a heating pad for pet snakes. Hamsters, gerbils, and other small rodents should be placed in a secure carrier. Bring bedding, food and water bowls, and food.

NOTES

[1] From How-To Survival Library, www.y2klibrary.com
[2] Ibid
[3] From "Helping Children Cope With Disaster." Developed by the Federal Emergency Management Agency and the American Red Cross.

REFERENCES AND RESOURCES

REFERENCE #1
PREPAREDNESS BOOKS

General

Making the Best of Basics: Family Preparedness Handbook
James Talmage Stevens
Paperback/February 1997
$22.95

Don't Get Caught With Your Pantry Down!: When the Unexpected Happens!
James T. Stevens/Lee Dee Jo Teaque-Stevens (Editor)
Paperback/May 1998
Historical Pubns/ISBN: 1-881825-19-1/$29.95

Beginner's Guide to Family Preparedness: Food Storage, Back to Basics, Survival Facts
Rosalie Mason
Paperback/June 1977
$11.98

101 Things to Do 'Til the Revolution: Ideas and Resources for Self-Liberation, Monkey Wrenching, and Preparedness
Claire Wolfe
Paperback/January 1999

Emergency Preparedness and First Aid Guide
Menasha Ridge Press/Paperback/October 1998/$12.95

Simply Ready: A Complete Guide for Provident Living and Personal Preparedness
Terri Johnson, Hans Johnson (Illustrator)
November 1998

Basic Preparedness: A 'How-To' Guide for Preparedness & Self-Reliant Living
Staff Survival Center/Paperback/July 1994
Survival Center Inc/ISBN: 0-964234-20-3

Eating Off the Grid: Storing and Cooking Foods Without Electricity
Denise Hansen MS RD
Spiral-bound/June 1, 1999
Subito Services/ISBN: 0-967139-40-6/$18.50

Beginners' Guide to Family Preparedness—Food Storage, Back to Basics, and Survival Facts
Rosalie Mason
Paperback/1977/$10.36
Emergency Preparedness
Boy Scouts of America Staff/Paperback/1999

Becoming Self-Reliant: How to Become Less Dependent on Society and the Government
Ken Larson
Paperback/1997

Blueprint for Crisis Preparedness
Anton Andereggen
Paperback/1989

Crisis Preparedness Handbook: A Comprehensive Guide to Home Storage & Physical Survival
Jack A. Spigareli
Paperback/1994

Disaster Can Happen Anywhere in the World! Are You Prepared?: The Complete Emergency & Disaster Preparedness Manual
Laura G. Kaplan and Lisa A. Moreland
Hardcover/1994

Disaster Preparedness Manual, 1998 Revision
Edward White, Robert Genovese, Trish Taylor
Hardcover 1998

Disaster Preparedness: A Bibliography
Mary Vance
Hardcover

Speciality Info

Earthquake Preparedness Guide: California Edition
Garrett M. Nelson, Eddie Braun
Trade Paperback

Awareness and Preparedness for Emergencies at a Local Level (Apell): A Process for Responding to Technological Accidents
United Nations/Paperback/January 1988

Disaster Preparedness Manual for Day Care Centers
Nicole L. Child
Paperback 1994

Earthquake & Disaster Preparedness: Surviving the Next Great Disaster
Eleanor Malin
Trade Paperback 1995/$7.96

Earthquake Preparedness for Office, Home, Family & Community
Libby Lafferty
Paperback 1994/$2.80

Be Ready, Be Safe for Earthquakes: A Child's Guide to Preparedness
Libby Lafferty, Tina Lafferty
Paperback 1994

Chemical Accident Safety: EPA's Responsibilities for Preparedness, Response, & Prevention
Trade Paperback 1996

Earthquake Public Information Materials: An Annotated Bibliography
Southern California Earthquake Preparedness Project Staff
Hardcover 1983

Hurricane Survival Made Easy: A Guide for Hurricane Preparedness
Morris I. Taite, Joe Masia
Paperback/July 1993

Earthquake Preparedness for Office, Home, Family, and Community
Libby Lafferty
Paperback/March 1996

Health & First Aid Info

Where There Is No Doctor: A Village Health Care Handbook
David Werner, Carol Thuman, Jane Maxwell
Paperback Revised/May 1992/
Hesperian Foundation/ISBN: 0-942364-15-5

Where There Is No Dentist
Murray Dickson
Paperback/June 1983/Hesperian Foundation/ISBN: 0-942364-05-8

Ditch Medicine: Advanced Field Procedures for Emergencies
Hugh L. Coffee
Paperback/May 1993/Paladin Press/ISBN: 0-873647-17-3/$25.00

U.S. Army Special Forces Medical Handbook/st 31-91B
U.S. Army Institute/Paperback/June 1987
Lyle Stuart/ISBN: 0-806510-45-5/$12.95

Do-It-Yourself Medicine
Ragnar Benson
Paperback/March 1997/Paladin Press/ISBN: 0-873649-18-4/$20.00

The American Medical Association Handbook of First Aid & Emergency Care
Stanley M. Zydio, James A. Hill (Editor),
Stanley M. Zydlo (Contributor)
$11.95 Paperback—332 pages Revised edition (September 1990)
Random House (Paper); ISBN: 0-679729-59-3

Emergency Medical Treatment: Infants, Children, and Adults: A Handbook on What to Do in an Emergency to Keep Someone Alive Until Help Arrives
Stephen N. Vogel, David Manhoff (Contributor)
Paperback/November 1993/Emt/ISBN: 0-916363-10-4/$12.95

Baby & Child Emergency First-Aid Handbook: Simple Step-By-Step Instructions for the Most Common Childhood Emergencies
Mitchell J. Einzig, M.D. (Editor)
Paperback/Revised edition/January 1995/$8.00
Meadowbrook Press/ISBN: 0-671519-76-X

REFERENCE #2
ORGANIZATIONS OFFERING DISASTER
PREPAREDNESS ASSISTANCE

FEMA (Federal Emergency Management Agency)
500 C Street
Washington, DC 20472
800-238-3358

Health and Human Services
901 D Street SW
Lafance Plaza Promade
Washington, DC 20001
202-401-9333

American Red Cross
1621 North Kent Street
Arlington, VA 22209
703-248-4222

American Foundation for the Blind (information and referral)
800-232-5463

National Institute on Deafness and Other Communication Disorders
800-241-1044

National Organization on Disabilities
202-293-5960

Disaster Websites

FEMA (Federal Emergency Management Agency)
   www.fema.gov

American Red Cross
   www.redcross.org

U.S. Organizations Dealing with Hazards and Disasters
www.olympus.net/personal/cline/statenat.html

The National Hazards Information Center (organizations that produce information about hazards and disasters)
hazctr@spot.colorado.edu

Contacts for Information Concerning Disaster/Emergency Preparedness in the Public Schools
http://ink.yahoo.com/bin/query?p=preparedness+schools&hc=o&hs=1

Survival Community and Action Groups in Hawaii
www.webpal.org/states/hw.htm

State by State Survival Community and Disaster Preparedness Groups
www.webpal.org/states/(your state abreviation).htm

Information Clearing House for Survival and Self-reliance
www.artrans.com/rmsg/city/daily.htm
www2.cybercities.com/a/aussurvivalist/survivalcontents.htm
www.artrans.com/rmsg/city/emerg.htm
www.artrans.com/rmsg/articles.htm

Survivalist Information Library (Project EPSILON)
wysiwyg://main.87/http://www.ezonline.com/ditto/howto.html
(Preparation at home)
www.ezonline.com/ditto/index.html
www.ezonline.com/ditto/texts/prepare.html

Homesteading and Small Farming Resource
www.homestead.org/framemain.htm

The Survival Library
www.netside.com/~lcoble/password/

Survival Groups
www2.cybercities.com/a/aussurvivalist/groups.htm

Survival Resources
www2.cybercities.com/a/aussurvivalist/online_res.htm

Common Sense Survival Guides
http://members.tripod.com/-sidlinger/
www.survival-center.com/guide/toc.htm

Survivalism Online
www.logicsouth.com/-lcoble/password/survival.html

Blue Wolf Survival and Preparedness
www.bwolf.com/

ANEW/Management Training, Survival Siminars, Outdoor Programs
www.ssurvival.com/

Wilderness Schools
www.geosmith.com/wilderness/schools.html

REFERENCE #3
DISASTER: HOUSE AND BUILDING FIRES

A fire can engulf a structure in a matter of minutes. Understanding the basic characteristics of fire and learning the proper safety practices can be the key to surviving a house or building fire.

Before

- Install smoke detectors. Check them once a month and change the batteries at least once a year. Develop and practice an escape plan. Make sure all family members know what to do in a fire.
- Draw a floor plan with at least two ways of escaping every room. Choose a safe meeting place outside the house. Practice alerting other household members. It is a good idea to keep a bell and a flashlight in each bedroom for this purpose.
- Practice evacuating the building blindfolded. In a real fire situation, the amount of smoke generated by a fire will most likely make it impossible to see.
- Practice staying low to the ground when escaping.
- Practice feeling all doors before opening them. If the door is hot, get out another way.
- Learn to stop, drop to the ground, and roll if clothes catch fire.
- Post emergency numbers near telephones. However, be aware that if a fire threatens your home, you should not place the call to your emergency services from inside the home. It is better to get out first and place the call from somewhere else.
- Purchase collapsible ladders at hardware stores and practice using them.
- Install A–B–C type fire extinguishers in the home and teach family members how to use them.
- Do not store combustible materials in closed areas or near a heat source.
- Check electrical wiring. Replace wiring if frayed or cracked.
- Make sure wiring is not under rugs, over nails, or in high traffic areas. Do not overload outlets or extension cords. Outlets should have cover plates and no exposed wiring.

- Only purchase appliances and electrical devices that have a label indicating that they have been inspected by a testing laboratory such as Underwriter's Laboratories (UL) or Factory Mutual (FM).
- Contact your local fire department or American Red Cross chapter for more information on fire safety.

HEATING DEVICES

Heating devices such as portable heaters, wood stoves, and fireplaces demand safe operation. Use portable heaters in well-ventilated rooms only.

Refuel kerosene heaters outdoors only. Have chimneys and wood stoves cleaned annually. Buy only approved heaters and follow the manufacturers' directions.

SMOKE DETECTORS

Smoke detectors more than double the chance of surviving a fire. Smoke detectors sense abnormal amounts of smoke or invisible combustion gases in the air. They can detect both smoldering and burning fires.

At least one smoke detector should be installed on every level of a structure. Test the smoke detectors each month and replace the batteries at least once a year. Purchase smoke detectors labeled by the Underwriter's Laboratories (UL) or Factory Mutual (FM).

COOKING

Keep the stove area clean and clear of combustibles such as bags, boxes, and other appliances. If a fire starts, put a lid over the burning pan or use a fire extinguisher. Be careful. Moving the pan can cause the fire to spread. Never pour water on grease fires.

During

- Get out as quickly and as safely as possible.
- Use the stairs to escape.
- When evacuating, stay low to the ground.
- If possible, cover mouth with a cloth to avoid inhaling smoke and gases.

- Close doors in each room after escaping to delay the spread of the fire.

If in a room with a closed door:
- If smoke is pouring in around the bottom of the door or it feels hot, keep the door closed.
- Open a window to escape or for fresh air while awaiting rescue.
- If there is no smoke at the bottom or top and the door is not hot, then open the door slowly.
- If there is too much smoke or fire in the hall, slam the door shut.
- Call the fire department from a location outside the house.

After

- Give first aid where appropriate.
- Seriously injured or burned victims should be transported to professional medical help immediately.
- Stay out of damaged buildings.
- Return home only when local fire authorities say it is safe.
- Look for structural damage.
- Discard food that has been exposed to heat, smoke, or soot.
- Contact insurance agent.
- Don't discard damaged goods until after an inventory has been taken. Save receipts for money relating to fire loss.

REFERENCE #4
DISASTER: FLOODS AND FLASH FLOODS

Mitigation pays. It includes any activities that prevent an emergency, reduce the chance of an emergency happening, or lessen the damaging effects of unavoidable emergencies. Investing in mitigation steps now, like constructing barriers such as levees and purchasing flood insurance will help reduce the amount of structural damage to your home and financial loss from building and crop damage should a flood or flash flood occur.

Before

- Find out if you live in a flood-prone area from your local emergency management office or Red Cross chapter. Ask whether your property is above or below the flood stage water level and learn about the history of flooding for your region.
- Learn flood warning signs and your community alert signals.
- Request information on preparing for floods and flash floods.
- If you live in a frequently flooded area, stockpile emergency building materials.These include plywood, plastic sheeting, lumber nails, hammer and saw, pry bar, shovels, and sandbags.
- Have check valves installed in building sewer traps to prevent flood waters from backing up in sewer drains. As a last resort, use large corks or stoppers to plug showers, tubs, or basins.
- Plan and practice an evacuation route.
- Contact the local emergency management office or local American Red Cross chapter for a copy of the community flood evacuation plan. This plan should include information on the safest routes to shelters.
- Individuals living in flash flood areas should have several alternative routes.
- Have disaster supplies on hand:
  - Flashlights and extra batteries
  - Portable, battery-operated radio and extra batteries
  - First aid kit and manual
  - Emergency food and water

- Nonelectric can opener
- Essential medicines
- Cash and credit cards
- Sturdy shoes

■ Develop an emergency communication plan. In case family members are separated from one another during floods or flashfloods (a real possibility during the day when adults are at work and children are at school), have a plan for getting back together.

■ Ask an out-of-state relative or friend to serve as the "family contact." After a disaster, it's often easier to call long distance. Make sure everyone in the family knows the name, address, and phone number of the contact person.

■ Make sure that all family members know how to respond after a flood or flash flood.

■ Teach all family members how and when to turn off gas, electricity, and water.

■ Teach children how and when to call 9-1-1, police, fire department, and which radio station to tune to for emergency information.

■ Learn about the National Flood Insurance Program.

■ Ask your insurance agent about flood insurance. Homeowners policies do not cover flood damage.

During a Flood Watch

■ Listen to a battery-operated radio for the latest storm information.

■ Fill bathtubs, sinks, and jugs with clean water in case water becomes contaminated.

■ Bring outdoor belongings, such as patio furniture, indoors.

■ Move valuable household possessions to the upper floors or to safe ground if time permits.

■ If you are instructed to do so by local authorities, turn off all utilities at the main switch and close the main gas valve.

■ Be prepared to evacuate.

During a Flood

IF INDOORS:

- Turn on battery-operated radio or television to get the latest emergency information.
- Get your preassembled emergency supplies.
- If told to leave, do so immediately.

IF OUTDOORS:

- Climb to high ground and stay there.
- Avoid walking through any floodwaters. If it is moving swiftly, even water 6 inches deep can sweep you off your feet.

IF IN A CAR:

- If you come to a flooded area, turn around and go another way.
- If your car stalls, abandon it immediately and climb to higher ground. Many deaths have resulted from attempts to move stalled vehicles.

During an Evacuation

- If advised to evacuate, do so immediately. Evacuation is much simpler and safer before flood waters become too deep for ordinary vehicles to drive through.
- Listen to a battery-operated radio for evacuation instructions.
- Follow recommended evacuation routes—shortcuts may be blocked.
- Leave early enough to avoid being marooned by flooded roads.

After

- Flood dangers do not end when the water begins to recede. Listen to a radio or television and don't return home until authorities indicate it is safe to do so.
- Remember to help your neighbors who may require special assistance—infants, elderly people, and people with disabilities.

- Inspect foundations for cracks or other damage.
- Stay out of buildings if flood waters remain around the building.
- When entering buildings, use extreme caution.
- Wear sturdy shoes and use battery—powered lanterns or flashlights when examining buildings.
- Examine walls, floors, doors, and windows to make sure that the building is not in danger of collapsing.
- Watch out for animals, especially poisonous snakes, that may have come into your home with the flood waters. Use a stick to poke through debris.
- Watch for loose plaster and ceilings that could fall.
- Take pictures of the damage—both to the house and its contents for insurance claims.
- Look for fire hazards:
  - Broken or leaking gas lines
  - Flooded electrical circuits
  - Submerged furnaces or electrical appliances
  - Flammable or explosive materials coming from upstream
- Throw away food—including canned goods—that has come in contact with flood waters.
- Pump out flooded basements gradually (about one-third of the water per day) to avoid structural damage.
- Service damaged septic tanks, cesspools, pits, and leaching systems as soon as possible. Damaged sewage systems are health hazards.

INSPECTING UTILITIES IN A DAMAGED HOME

- Check for gas leaks—If you smell gas or hear a blowing or hissing noise, open a window and quickly leave the building. Turn off the gas at the outside main valve if you can and call the gas company from a neighbor's home. If you turn off the gas for any reason, it must be turned back on by a professional.
- Look for electrical system damage—If you see sparks or broken or frayed wires, or if you smell hot insulation, turn off the electricity at the main fuse box or circuit breaker.

- If you have to step in water to get to the fuse box or circuit breaker, call an electrician for advice.
- Check for sewage and water lines damage—if you suspect sewage lines are damaged avoid using the toilets and call a plumber.
- If water pipes are damaged, contact the water company and avoid the water from the tap. You can obtain safe water by melting ice cubes.

REFERENCE #5
DISASTER: HURRICANES

Hurricanes can be dangerous killers. Learning the hurricane warning messages and planning ahead can reduce the chances of injury or major property damage.

Before

- Plan an evacuation route.
- Contact the local emergency management office or American Red Cross chapter, and ask for the community hurricane preparedness plan. This plan should include information on the safest evacuation routes and nearby shelters.
- Learn safe routes inland.
- Be ready to drive 20 to 50 miles inland to locate a safe place.
- Have disaster supplies on hand:
  - Flashlight and extra batteries
  - Portable, battery-operated radio and extra batteries
  - First aid kit and manual
  - Emergency food and water
  - Nonelectric can opener
  - Essential medicines
  - Cash and credit cards
  - Sturdy shoes
- Make arrangements for pets. Pets may not be allowed into emergency shelters for health and space reasons. Contact your local humane society for information on local animal shelters.
- Make sure that all family members know how to respond after a hurricane. Teach family members how and when to turn off gas, electricity, and water.
- Teach children how and when to call 9-1-1, police, or fire department and which radio station to tune to for emergency information.
- Protect your windows. Permanent shutters are the best protection. A lower-cost approach is to put up plywood panels. Use 1/2 inch plywood—marine plywood is best—cut to fit each window.

Remember to mark which board fits which window. Pre-drill
holes every 18 inches for screws. Do this long before the storm.
- Trim back dead or weak branches from trees.
- Check into flood insurance. You can find out about the National
  Flood Insurance Program through your local insurance agent or
  emergency management office.There is normally a 30-day waiting period before a new policy becomes effective. Homeowners'
  polices do not cover damage from the flooding that accompanies
  a hurricane.
- Develop an emergency communication plan.
- In case family members are separated from one another during a
  disaster (a real possibility during the day when adults are at work
  and children are at school), have a plan for getting back together.
- Ask an out-of-state relative or friend to serve as the "family contact." After a disaster, it's often easier to call long distance. Make
  sure everyone in the family knows the name, address, and
  phone number of the contact person.

MITIGATION

Mitigation includes any activities that prevent an emergency, reduce
the chance of an emergency happening, or lessen the damaging
effects of unavoidable emergencies. Investing in preventive mitigation
steps now such as strengthening unreinforced masonry to withstand
wind and flooding and installing shutters on every window will help
reduce the impact of hurricanes in the future.

For more information on mitigation, contact your local emergency
management office.

HURRICANE WATCHES AND WARNINGS

A hurricane watch is issued when there is a threat of hurricane conditions within 24–36 hours. A hurricane warning is issued when hurricane conditions (winds of 74 miles per hour or greater, or dangerously
high water and rough seas) are expected in 24 hours or less.

DURING A HURRICANE WATCH

- Listen to a battery-operated radio or television for hurricane progress reports.
- Check emergency supplies.
- Fuel car.
- Bring in outdoor objects such as lawn furniture, toys, and garden tools and anchor objects that cannot be brought inside.
- Secure buildings by closing and boarding up windows. Remove outside antennas.
- Turn refrigerator and freezer to coldest settings. Open only when absolutely necessary and close quickly.
- Store drinking water in clean bathtubs, jugs, bottles, and cooking containers.
- Review evacuation plan.
- Moor boat securely or move it to a designated safe place. Use rope or chain to secure boat to trailer. Use tiedowns to anchor trailer to the ground or house.

DURING A HURRICANE WARNING

- Listen constantly to a battery-operated radio or television for official instructions.
- If in a mobile home, check tiedowns and evacuate immediately.
- Store valuables and personal papers in a waterproof container on the highest level of your home.
- Avoid elevators.

If at home:
- Stay inside, away from windows, skylights, and glass doors.
- Keep a supply of flashlights and extra batteries handy. Avoid open flames, such as candles and kerosene lamps, as a source of light.
- If power is lost, turn off major appliances to reduce power "surge" when electricity is restored.

If officials indicate evacuation is necessary:
- Leave as soon as possible. Avoid flooded roads and watch for washed-out bridges.

- Secure your home by unplugging appliances and turning off electricity and the main water valve.
- Tell someone outside of the storm area where you are going.
- If time permits, and you live in an identified surge zone, elevate furniture to protect it from flooding or better yet, move it to a higher floor.
- Bring preassembled emergency supplies and warm protective clothing.
- Take blankets and sleeping bags to shelter.
- Lock up home and leave.

After

- Stay tuned to local radio for information.
- Help injured or trapped persons.
- Give first aid where appropriate. Do not move seriously injured persons unless they are in immediate danger of further injury. Call for help.
- Return home only after authorities advise that it is safe to do so.
- Avoid loose or dangling power lines and report them immediately to the power company, police, or fire department.
- Enter your home with caution.
- Beware of snakes, insects, and animals driven to higher ground by flood water.
- Open windows and doors to ventilate and dry your home.
- Check refrigerated foods for spoilage.
- Take pictures of the damage, both to the house and its contents for insurance claims.
- Drive only if absolutely necessary and avoid flooded roads and washed-out bridges.
- Use telephone only for emergency calls.

INSPECTING UTILITIES IN A DAMAGED HOME

- Check for gas leaks—If you smell gas or hear a blowing or hissing noise, open a window and quickly leave the building. Turn off the gas at the outside main valve if you can and call the gas company from a neighbor's home. If you turn off the gas for any reason, it must be turned back on by a professional.

- Look for electrical system damage—If you see sparks or broken or frayed wires, or if you smell hot insulation, turn off the electricity at the main fuse box or circuit breaker. If you have to step in water to get to the fuse box or circuit breaker, call an electrician first for advice.

- Check for sewage and water lines damage—If you suspect sewage lines are damaged avoid using the toilets and call a plumber.

- If water pipes are damaged, contact the water company and avoid the water from the tap. You can obtain safe water by melting ice cubes.

REFERENCE #6
DISASTER: THUNDERSTORMS
AND LIGHTNING

Some thunderstorms can be seen approaching, while others hit without warning. It is important to learn to recognize the danger signs and to plan ahead.

Before

- Learn the thunderstorm danger signs.
  - Dark, towering, or threatening clouds
  - Distant lightning and thunder
- Have disaster supplies on hand.
  - Flashlight with extra batteries
  - Portable, battery-operated radio and extra batteries
  - First aid kit and manual
  - Emergency food and water
  - Nonelectric can opener
  - Essential medicines
  - Cash and credit cards
  - Sturdy shoes
- Check for hazards in the yard.
- Dead or rotting trees and branches can fall during a severe thunderstorm and cause injury and damage.
- Make sure that all family members know how to respond after a thunderstorm.
- Teach family members how and when to turn off gas, electricity, and water.
- Teach children how and when to call 9-1-1, police, fire department, and which radio station to tune to for emergency information.

SEVERE THUNDERSTORM WATCHES AND WARNINGS

A severe thunderstorm watch is issued by the National Weather Service when the weather conditions are such that a severe thunderstorm (damaging winds 58 miles per hour or more, or hail three-fourths of an inch in diameter or greater) is likely to develop. This is the time to locate a safe place in the home and tell family members to watch the sky and listen to the radio for more information.

A severe thunderstorm warning is issued when a severe thunderstorm has been sighted or indicated by weather radar. At this point, the danger is very serious and everyone should go to a safe place, turn on a battery-operated radio, and wait for the "all clear" by the authorities.

Learn how to respond to a tornado and flash flood. Tornadoes are spawned by thunderstorms, and flash flooding can occur with thunderstorms. When a "severe thunderstorm warning" is issued, review what actions to take under a "tornado warning" or a "flash flood warning."

DEVELOP AN EMERGENCY COMMUNICATION PLAN

- In case family members are separated from one another during a thunderstorm (a real possibility during the day when adults are at work and children are at school), have a plan for getting back together.
- Ask an out-of-state relative or friend to serve as the "family contact." After a disaster, it's often easier to call long distance. Make sure everyone knows the name, address, and phone number of the contact person.
- Contact your local emergency management office or American Red Cross chapter for more information on thunderstorms and lightning.

MITIGATION

Mitigation includes any activities that prevent an emergency, reduce the chance of an emergency happening, or lessen the damaging effects of unavoidable emergencies. Investing in preventive mitigation steps now, such as installing lightning rods to carry the electrical charge of lightning bolts safely to the ground or purchasing flood insurance, will help reduce the impact of severe thunderstorms in the future. For more information on mitigation, contact your local emergency management office.

During

IF INDOORS:

- Secure outdoor objects such as lawn furniture that could blow away or cause damage or injury. Take light objects inside.
- Shutter windows securely and brace outside doors.
- Listen to a battery-operated radio for the latest storm information.
- Do not handle any electrical equipment or telephones because lightning could follow the wire. Television sets are particularly dangerous at this time.
- Avoid bathtubs, water faucets, and sinks because metal pipes can transmit electricity.

IF OUTDOORS:

- Attempt to get into a building or car.
- If no structure is available, get to an open space and squat low to the ground as quickly as possible. (If in the woods, find an area protected by a low clump of trees—never stand underneath a single large tree in the open.)
- Be aware of the potential for flooding in low-lying areas.
- Avoid tall structures such as towers, tall trees, fences, telephone lines, or power lines.
- Stay away from natural lightning rods such as golf clubs, tractors, fishing rods, bicycles, or camping equipment.
- Stay away from rivers, lakes, or other bodies of water.
- If you are isolated in a level field or prairie and you feel your hair stand on end (which indicates that lightning is about to strike), bend forward, putting your hands on your knees. A position with feet together and crouching while removing all metal objects is recommended. Do not lie flat on the ground.

IF IN A CAR:

- Pull safely onto the shoulder of the road away from any trees that could fall on the vehicle.

- Stay in the car and turn on the emergency flashers until the heavy rains subside.
- Avoid flooded roadways.

ESTIMATING THE DISTANCE FROM A THUNDERSTORM

Because light travels much faster than sound, lightning flashes can be seen long before the resulting thunder is heard. Estimate the number of miles you are from a thunderstorm by counting the number of seconds between a flash of lightning and the next clap of thunder. Divide this number by five.

Important: *You are in danger from lightning if you can hear thunder.*
Knowing how far away a storm is does not mean that you're in danger only when the storm is overhead.

HAIL

Hail is produced by many strong thunderstorms. Hail can be smaller than a pea or as large as a softball and can be very destructive to plants and crops.

In a hailstorm, take cover immediately. Pets and livestock are particularly vulnerable to hail, so bring animals into a shelter.

After

- Check for injuries.
- A person who has been struck by lightning does not carry an electrical charge that can shock other people. If the victim is burned, provide first aid and call emergency medical assistance immediately.
- Look for burns where lightning entered and exited the body. If the strike caused the victim's heart and breathing to stop, give cardiopulmonary resuscitation (CPR) until medical professionals arrive and take over.
- Remember to check on people that may need assistance—infants, elderly people, and people with disabilities.
- Report downed utility wires.
- Drive only if necessary. Debris and washed-out roads may make driving dangerous.

REFERENCE #7
DISASTER: TORNADOES

When a tornado is coming, you have only a short amount of time to make life-or-death decisions. Advance planning and quick response are the keys to surviving a tornado.

Before

- Conduct tornado drills each tornado season.
- Designate an area in the home as a shelter, and practice having everyone in the family go there in response to a tornado threat.
- Discuss with family members the difference between a "tornado watch" and a "tornado warning."
- Contact your local emergency management office or American Red Cross chapter for more information on tornadoes.
- Have disaster supplies on hand.
  - Flashlight and extra batteries
  - Portable, battery-operated radio and extra batteries
  - First aid kit and manual
  - Emergency food and water
  - Nonelectric can opener
  - Essential medicines
  - Cash and credit cards
  - Sturdy shoes
- Develop an emergency communication plan.
- In case family members are separated from one another during a tornado (a real possibility during the day when adults are at work and children are at school), have a plan for getting back together.
- Ask an out-of-state relative or friend to serve as the "family contact." After a disaster, it's often easier to call long distance. Make sure everyone in the family knows the name, address, and phone number of the contact person.

TORNADO WATCHES AND WARNINGS

A tornado watch is issued by the National Weather Service when tornadoes are possible in your area. Remain alert for approaching storms. This is time to remind family members where the safest places within your home are located, and listen to the radio or television for further developments.

A tornado warning is issued when a tornado has been sighted or indicated by weather radar.

MOBILE HOMES

Mobile homes are particularly vulnerable. A mobile home can overturn very easily even if precautions have been taken to tie down the unit. When a tornado warning is issued, take shelter in a building with a strong foundation. If shelter is not available, lie in a ditch or low-lying area a safe distance away from the unit.

TORNADO DANGER SIGNS

- An approaching cloud of debris can mark the location of a tornado even if a funnel is not visible.
- Before a tornado hits, the wind may die down and the air may become very still.
- Tornadoes generally occur near the trailing edge of a thunderstorm.
- It is not uncommon to see clear, sunlit skies behind a tornado.

MITIGATION

Mitigation includes any activities that prevent an emergency, reduce the chance of an emergency happening, or lessen the damaging effects of unavoidable emergencies. Investing in preventive mitigation steps now, such as checking local building codes and ordinances about wind-resistant designs and strengthening unreinforced masonry, will help reduce the impact of tornadoes in the future. For more information on mitigation, contact your local emergency management office.

During

IF AT HOME:

- Go at once to the basement, storm cellar, or the lowest level of the building.
- If there is no basement, go to an inner hallway or a smaller inner room without windows, such as a bathroom or closet.
- Get away from the windows.
- Go to the center of the room.
- Stay away from corners because they tend to attract debris.
- Get under a piece of sturdy furniture such as a workbench or heavy table or desk and hold on to it.
- Use arms to protect head and neck.
- If in a mobile home, get out and find shelter elsewhere.

IF AT WORK OR SCHOOL:

- Go to the basement or to an inside hallway at the lowest level.
- Avoid places with wide-span roofs such as auditoriums, cafeterias, large hallways, or shopping malls.
- Get under a piece of sturdy furniture such as a workbench or heavy table or desk and hold on to it.
- Use arms to protect head and neck.

IF OUTDOORS:

- If possible, get inside a building.
- If shelter is not available or there is no time to get indoors, lie in a ditch or low-lying area or crouch near a strong building. Be aware of the potential for flooding.
- Use arms to protect head and neck.

IF IN A CAR:

- Never try to out drive a tornado in a car or truck. A tornado can quickly change direction and grab a car and toss it through the air.
- Get out of the car immediately and take shelter in a nearby building.

- If there is no time to get indoors, get out of the car and lie in a ditch or low-lying area away from the vehicle. Be aware of the potential for flooding.

After

- Help injured or trapped persons.
- Give first aid when appropriate. Don't try to move the seriously injured unless they are in immediate danger of further injury. Call for help.
- Turn on radio or television to get the latest emergency information.
- Stay out of damaged buildings. Return home only when authorities say it is safe.
- Use the telephone only for emergency calls.
- Clean up spilled medicines, bleaches, or gasoline or other flammable liquids immediately.
- Leave the buildings if you smell gas or chemical fumes.
- Take pictures of the damage—both of the house and its contents—for insurance purposes.
- Remember to help your neighbors who may require special assistance—infants, the elderly, and people with disabilities.

INSPECTING UTILITIES IN A DAMAGED HOME

- Check for gas leaks—If you smell gas or hear a blowing or hissing noise, open a window and quickly leave the building. Turn off the gas at the outside main valve if you can and call the gas company from a neighbor's home. If you turn off the gas for any reason, it must be turned back on by a professional.
- Look for electrical system damage—If you see sparks or broken or frayed wires, or if you smell hot insulation, turn off the electricity at the main fuse box or circuit breaker. If you have to step in water to get to the fuse box or circuit breaker, call an electrician first for advice.
- Check for sewage and water lines damage—If you suspect sewage lines are damaged, avoid using toilets and call a plumber. If water pipes are damaged, contact the water company and avoid using water from the tap. You can obtain safe water by melting ice cubes.

Fujita–Pearson Tornado Scale

F-0	40–72 mph	chimney damage, tree branches broken
F-1	73–112 mph	mobile homes pushed off foundation or overturned
F-2	113–157 mph	considerable damage, mobile homes demolished, trees uprooted
F-3	158–205 mph	roofs and walls torn down, trains overturned, cars thrown
F-4	207–260 mph	well-constructed walls leveled
F-5	261–318 mph	homes lifted off foundation and carried considerable distances, autos thrown as far as 100 meters

REFERENCE #8
DISASTER: EARTHQUAKES
(From Federal Emergency Management Agency-FEMA)

Earthquakes strike suddenly, violently, and without warning. Identifying potential hazards ahead of time and advance planning can reduce the dangers of serious injury or loss of life from an earthquake.

Before

- Fasten shelves securely to walls.
- Place large or heavy objects on lower shelves.
- Store breakable items such as bottled foods, glass, and china in low, closed cabinets with latches.
- Hang heavy items such as pictures and mirrors away from beds, couches, and anywhere people sit.
- Brace overhead light fixtures.
- Repair defective electrical wiring and leaky gas connections. These are potential fire risks.
- Secure a water heater by strapping it to the wall studs and bolting it to the floor.
- Repair any deep cracks in ceilings or foundations. Get expert advice if there are signs of structural defects.
- Store weed killers, pesticides, and flammable products securely in closed cabinets with latches and on bottom shelves.
- Identify safe places in each room:
  - Under sturdy furniture such as a heavy desk or table
  - Against an inside wall
  - Away from where glass could shatter around windows, mirrors, pictures, or where heavy bookcases or other heavy furniture could fall over
- Locate safe places outdoors: in the open, away from buildings, trees, telephone and electrical lines, overpasses, or elevated expressways.

- Make sure all family members know how to respond after an earthquake. Teach family members how and when to turn off gas, electricity, and water.
- Teach children how and when to call 9-1-1, police, or fire department and which radio station to tune to for emergency information.
- Contact your local emergency management office or American Red Cross chapter for more information on earthquakes.
- Have disaster supplies on hand:
  - Flashlight and extra batteries
  - Portable battery-operated radio and extra batteries
  - First aid kit and manual
  - Emergency food and water
  - Nonelectric can opener
  - Essential medicines
  - Cash and credit cards
  - Sturdy shoes
- Develop an emergency communication plan. In case family members are separated from one another during an earthquake (a real possibility during the day when adults are at work and children are at school), develop a plan for reuniting after the disaster.
- Ask an out-of-state relative or friend to serve as the "family contact." After a disaster, it's often easier to call long distance. Make sure everyone in the family knows the name, address, and phone number of the contact person.

MITIGATION

Mitigation includes any activities that prevent an emergency, reduce the chance of an emergency happening, or lessen the damaging effects of unavoidable emergencies. Investing in preventive mitigation steps now, such as repairing deep plaster cracks in ceilings and foundations, anchoring overhead lighting fixtures to the ceiling and following local seismic building standards, will help reduce the impact of earthquakes in the future. For more information on mitigation, contact your local emergency management office.

During

IF INDOORS:

- Take cover under a piece of heavy furniture or against an inside wall and hold on.
- Stay inside.
- The most dangerous thing to do during the shaking of an earthquake is to try to leave the building because objects can fall on you.

IF OUTDOORS:

- Move into the open, away from buildings, street lights, and utility wires.
- Once in the open, stay there until the shaking stops.

IF IN A MOVING VEHICLE:

- Move to a clear area away from buildings, trees, overpasses, or utility wires. Stop as quickly as possible and stay in the vehicle.
- Once the shaking has stopped, proceed with caution. Avoid bridges or ramps that might have been damaged by the quake.

After

- Be prepared for aftershocks. Although smaller than the main shock, aftershocks cause additional damage and may bring weakened structures down.
- Aftershocks can occur in the first hours, days, weeks, or even months after the quake.
- Help injured or trapped persons. Give first aid where appropriate. Do not move seriously injured persons unless they are in immediate danger of further injury. Call for help.
- Listen to a battery-operated radio or television for the latest emergency information.
- Remember to help your neighbors who may require special assistance—infants, the elderly, and people with disabilities.
- Stay out of damaged buildings. Return home only when authorities say it is safe.

- Use the telephone only for emergency calls.
- Clean up spilled medicines, bleaches, or gasoline or other flammable liquids immediately. Leave the area if you smell gas or fumes from other chemicals.
- Open closet and cupboard doors cautiously.
- Inspect the entire length of chimneys carefully for damage. Unnoticed damage could lead to a fire.

INSPECTING UTILITIES IN A DAMAGED HOME

- Check for gas leaks—If you smell gas or hear a blowing or hissing noise, open a window and quickly leave the building. Turn off the gas at the outside main valve if you can and call the gas company from a neighbor's home. If you turn off the gas for any reason, it must be turned back on by a professional.
- Look for electrical system damage—If you see sparks or broken or frayed wires, or if you smell hot insulation, turn off the electricity at the main fuse box or circuit breaker. If you have to step in water to get to the fuse box or circuit breaker, call an electrician first for advice.
- Check for sewage and water lines damage—If you suspect sewage lines are damaged, avoid using the toilets and call a plumber. If water pipes are damaged, contact the water company and avoid using water from the tap. You can obtain safe water by melting ice cubes.

PETS AFTER AN EARTHQUAKE

The behavior of pets may change dramatically after an earthquake. Normally quiet and friendly cats and dogs may become aggressive or defensive. Watch animals closely. Leash dogs and place them in a fenced yard. Pets may not be allowed into shelters for health and space reasons. Prepare an emergency pen for pets in the home that includes a 3-day supply of dry food and a large container of water.

REFERENCE #9
DISASTER: WINTER STORMS

A major winter storm can be lethal. Preparing for cold weather conditions and responding to them effectively can reduce the dangers caused by winter storms.

Before

- Be familiar with winter storm warning messages.
- Service snow removal equipment and have rock salt on hand to melt ice on walkways and kitty litter to generate temporary traction.
- Make sure you have sufficient heating fuel; regular fuel sources may be cut off.
- Winterize your home.
  - Insulate walls and attic.
  - Caulk and weather-strip doors and windows.
  - Install storm windows or cover windows with plastic from the inside.
- Have safe emergency heating equipment available.
  - Fireplace with ample supply of wood
  - Small, well-vented, wood, coal, or camp stove with fuel
  - Portable space heaters or kerosene heaters (see Kerosene Heaters, below)
- Install and check smoke detectors.
- Contact your local emergency management office or American Red Cross chapter for more information on winter storms.
- Keep pipes from freezing. Wrap pipes in insulation or layers of old newspapers. Cover the newspapers with plastic to keep out moisture. Let faucets drip a little to avoid freezing.
- Know how to shut off water valves.
- Have disaster supplies on hand, in case the power goes out.
  - Flashlight and extra batteries
  - Portable, battery-operated radio and extra batteries
  - First aid kit
  - One-week supply of food (include items that do not require refrigeration or cooking in case the power is shut off)

- Nonelectric can opener
- One-week supply of essential prescription medications
- Extra blankets and sleeping bags
- Fire extinguisher (A–B–C type)
- Develop an emergency communication plan.
- In case family members are separated from one another during a winter storm (a real possibility during the day when adults are at work and children are at school), have a plan for getting back together.
- Ask an out-of-state relative or friend to serve as the "family contact." After a disaster, it's often easier to call long distance. Make sure everyone knows the name, address, and phone number of the contact person.
- Make sure that all family members know how to respond after a severe winter storm.
- Teach children how and when to call 9-1-1, police, or fire department, and which radio station to tune to for emergency information.

KEROSENE HEATERS

- Check with your local fire department on the legality of using kerosene heaters in your community.
- Use only the correct fuel for your unit and follow the manufacturer's instructions.
- Refuel outdoors only, and only when cool. Keep your kerosene heater at least 3 feet away from furniture and other flammable objects.

MITIGATION

Mitigation includes any activities that prevent an emergency, reduce the chance of an emergency happening, or lessen the damaging effects of unavoidable emergencies. Investing in preventive mitigation steps now such as purchasing a flood insurance policy and installing storm windows will help reduce the impact of winter storms in the future. For more information on mitigation, contact your local emergency management office.

During

IF INDOORS:

- Stay indoors and dress warmly.
- Conserve fuel. Lower the thermostat to 65 degrees during the day and 55 degrees at night. Close off unused rooms.
- If the pipes freeze, remove any insulation or layers of newspapers and wrap pipes in rags.
- Completely open all faucets and pour hot water over the pipes, starting where they were most exposed to the cold (or where the cold was most likely to penetrate).
- Listen to the radio or television to get the latest information.

IF OUTDOORS:

- Dress warmly.
- Wear loose-fitting, layered, light-weight clothing. Layers can be removed to prevent perspiration and chill. Outer garments should be tightly woven and water repellent. Mittens are warmer than gloves because fingers generate warmth when they touch each other.
- Stretch before you go out.
- If you go out to shovel snow, do a few stretching exercises to warm up your body. Also take frequent breaks.
- Protect your lungs from extremely cold air by covering your mouth when outdoors. Try not to speak unless absolutely necessary.
- Avoid overexertion. Cold weather puts an added strain on the heart. Unaccustomed exercise such as shoveling snow or pushing a car can bring on a heart attack or make other medical conditions worse. Be aware of symptoms of dehydration.
- Watch for signs of frostbite and hypothermia.
- Keep dry. Change wet clothing frequently to prevent a loss of body heat. Wet clothing loses all of its insulating value and transmits heat rapidly.
- Remember to help your neighbors who may require special assistance—infants, elderly people, and people with disabilities.

WIND CHILL

"Wind chill" is a calculation of how cold it feels outside when the effects of temperature and wind speed are combined. A strong wind combined with a temperature of just below freezing can have the same effect as a still air temperature about 35 degrees colder.

WINTER STORM WATCHES AND WARNINGS

A winter storm watch indicates that severe winter weather may affect your area.

A winter storm warning indicates that severe winter weather conditions are definitely on the way.

A blizzard warning means that large amounts of falling or blowing snow and sustained winds of at least 35 miles per hour are expected for several hours.

FROSTBITE AND HYPOTHERMIA

Frostbite is a severe reaction to cold exposure that can permanently damage its victims. A loss of feeling and a white or pale appearance in fingers, toes, nose, or ear lobes are symptoms of frostbite.

Hypothermia is a condition brought on when the body temperature drops to less than 90 degrees Fahrenheit. Symptoms of hypothermia include uncontrollable shivering, slow speech, memory lapses, frequent stumbling, drowsiness, and exhaustion.

If frostbite or hypothermia is suspected, begin warming the person slowly and seek immediate medical assistance.

Warm the person's trunk first. Use your own body heat to help. Arms and legs should be warmed last because stimulation of the limbs can drive cold blood toward the heart and lead to heart failure. Put person in dry clothing and wrap his or her entire body in a blanket.

Never give a frostbite or hypothermia victim something with caffeine in it (like coffee or tea) or alcohol. Caffeine, a stimulant, can cause the heart to beat faster and hasten the effects the cold has on the body. Alcohol, a depressant, can slow the heart and also hasten the ill effects of cold body temperatures.

COLD WEATHER ISSUES

(From How-To Survival Library, www.y2klibrary.com)

Summary of Conditions:

WET COLD

Wet cold conditions occur where variations in day and night temperatures cause alternate freezing and thawing. These conditions are often accompanied by wet snow and rain causing the ground to become slushy and muddy. Wet cold requires clothing with a waterproof or water-repellent, wind-resistant outer layer, and an insulated inner layer sufficient for moderately cold weather of 14°F and above. Waterproof footwear is essential.

DRY COLD

Dry cold conditions occur when average temperatures are lower than 14° F. The ground is usually frozen and the snow dry. These low temperatures and wind increase the need to protect the entire body. Dry cold requires layered clothing that insulates against a wind-chill. The inner layers of insulation must be protected by a water-repellent, wind-resistant outer layer.

INTENSE COLD

Intense cold air temperatures (–5 to –25°F) are in the range where materials begin to change, adversely affecting operations. Fuels gel, back blast areas triple, artillery fires drop 100 per 1000 meters, water in containers freezes quickly. Appropriate protective clothing is required.

EXTREME COLD

Extreme cold (below –25°F) inhibits full-scale combat. Special fuels and lubricants are required, rubber becomes stiff and brittle, and close tolerances are affected. Operator personnel must have special protection from the elements.

Survival

Water, Food, Shelter
Protective clothing
Will to survive
Training/equipment
60–80% of body heat is lost through the head

Remember "COLD" is the key to keeping warm in cold weather:

Clean clothing
Overheating
Loose, layered clothes
Dry clothing

Overheating can cause perspiration which can lead to hypothermia in cold weather situations.

Cold Weather Injuries

NON FREEZING:
Hypothermia
Dehydration
Trench foot
Immersion Foot
FREEZING:
Frostbite

FACTORS THAT INFLUENCE COLD WEATHER INJURIES (CWI)

Previous CWI
Race
Geological Origin
Ambient Temperature
Wind Chill Factor
Type of Mission
Terrain
Nutrition
Alcohol, Drugs, Tobacco

Clothing
Moisture
Dehydration
Age
Fatigue
Other Injury
Discipline
Activity
Sharp Changes in Weather

PREVENTION OF COLD WEATHER INJURIES

Training
Planning
Weather Data
Foot Care
Proper Use of Gloves/Headgear
Proper Undergarments

HYPOTHERMIA

Hypothermia is when your body's heat loss exceeds the rate that your body can produce it. Your body can produce only a limited amount of heat to keep yourself warm. When your body is producing as much heat as it can and your body temperature is still lowering, you are suffering from hypothermia. Hypothermia can occur no matter what the temperature is. It is important to know the symptoms and treatment for hypothermia.

Causes:
- Heat loss exceeds heat production
- Wind/water chill
- Radiation—heat like light
- Conduction—sitting on cold surface—handling cold objects
- Convection—wind/water
- Evaporation—wet clothing
- Respiration—breathing cold air

Symptoms:
- Intense shivering
- Feeling of deep/cold numbness
- Muscle tensing
- Fatigue
- Poor coordination
- Disorientation
- Blueness of skin
- Slow, weak, irregular pulse
- Slurred speech
- Retreat inward psychologically
- Dullness
- Apathy

Treatment:
- Immediately raise body temperature
- Shelter from wind and weather
- Insulate from ground
- Replace wet clothing with dry
- Increase exercise if possible
- Give hot drinks and food
- Get in warm sleeping bag
- Shared body warmth
- Hot packs/hand warmers under armpits and groin area

DEHYDRATION

Cause:
- Not consuming as much water as the body uses

Symptoms of normal dehydration:
- Higher temperature
- Poor skin color
- Upset stomach
- Dizziness
- Weakness

- Confusion
- Dryness of mouth and throat
- Difficulty swallowing

Symptoms of SEVERE dehydration:
- Similar to hypothermia

Typical hypothermia/dehydration differentiation test:
- Warm belly—dehydration
- Cold belly—hypothermia

Cold weather dehydration can lead to total body core cooling.

TRENCH FOOT

Cause:
- Exposure to wet and cold around freezing

Symptoms:
- Feet and toes are pale and numb, cold, and stiff

Note:
- If preventive action is not taken at this stage feet will swell and become painful!

Treatment:
- Do NOT rub or massage
- Clean carefully with soap and water if indoors
- Dry, elevate, and expose to room temperature
- Stay off feet and replace socks

IMMERSION FOOT

Cause:
- Prolonged immersion in cold water < 50°F or in wet footwear > 12 hours. Aching and stinging pain on prolonged exposure.
- Initially no unusual

Symptoms:
- Sensations of pain. Skin becomes shriveled and soft.

Note:
- Handle gently—same as trench foot.

FROSTBITE

Cause:
- Freezing of skin or tissues due to exposure to temperatures at or below freezing, commonly by exposure to liquids that freeze at low temperatures such as gasoline, cleaning solvents, and salt water, or high velocity wind flow or metal surfaces.
- *Exposure can occur in minutes!*
- Wind or contact with wet clothing may produce an effective temperature in freezing range when air temperature is above freezing.

Symptoms:
- First degree: Aching, tingling sensation with cold and numbness. Skin usually turns red.
- Second degree: Pale grey and waxy white.
- Third degree: Black—no feeling no blood flow

Treatment:
- Handle gently—same as trench foot. DO NOT use water to warm affected areas.

> CHEEKS: Cover with warm hands until pain returns
> FINGERS: Place uncovered under arm pits or belly next to skin.
> FEET: Bare feet against belly of companion, under clothing, avoid rubbing or massaging. Don't pop blisters!
> CLOTHING: DRY, and proper for weather.
> EXERCISE: Routine exercise of face, fingers, and toes.

REFERENCE #10
DISASTER: NUCLEAR POWER PLANT EMERGENCY

Since 1980, each utility that owns a commercial nuclear power plant in the United States has been required to have both an onsite and off-site emergency response plan as a condition of obtaining and maintaining a license to operate that plant. Onsite emergency response plans are approved by the Nuclear Regulatory Commission (NRC). Offsite plans (which are closely coordinated with the utility's onsite emergency response plan) are evaluated by the Federal Emergency Management Agency (FEMA) and provided to the NRC, who must consider the FEMA findings when issuing or maintaining a license.

Federal law establishes the criteria for determining the adequacy of offsite planning and preparedness: "Plans and preparedness must be determined to adequately protect the public health and safety by providing reasonable assurance that appropriate measures can be taken offsite in the event of a radiological emergency."

Although construction and operation of nuclear power plants are closely monitored and regulated by the NRC, an accident, though unlikely, is possible. There is potential danger from an exposure to radiation. This exposure could come from the release of radioactive material from the plant into the environment, usually characterized by a plume (cloud-like) formation. The area the radioactive release may affect is determined by the amount released from the plant, wind direction and speed, and weather conditions (i.e., rain, snow, etc.) which would quickly drive the radioactive material to the ground, hence causing increased deposition of radionuclides.

If a release of radiation occurs, the levels of radioactivity will be monitored by authorities from Federal and State governments, and the utility, to determine the potential danger in order to protect the public.

What Is Radiation?

Radiation is any form of energy propagated as rays, waves, or energetic particles that travel through the air or a material medium. Radioactive materials are composed of atoms that are unstable. An unstable atom gives off its excess energy until it becomes stable. The energy emitted is radiation. The process by which an atom changes from an unstable state to a more stable state by emitting radiation is called radioactive decay or radioactivity.

People receive some natural or background radiation exposure each day from the sun, radioactive elements in the soil and rocks, household appliances (like television sets and microwave ovens), and medical and dental x-rays. Even the human body itself emits radiation. These levels of natural and background radiation is normal. The average American receives 360 millirems of radiation each year, 300 from natural sources and 60 from man-made activities. (A rem is a unit of radiation exposure.)

Radioactive materials—if handled improperly—or radiation accidentally released into the environment can be dangerous because of the harmful effects of certain types of radiation on the body. The longer a person is exposed to radiation and the closer the person is to the radiation, the greater the risk.

Although radiation cannot be detected by the senses (sight, smell, etc.), it is easily detected by scientists with sophisticated instruments that can detect even the smallest levels of radiation.

Preparing For an Emergency

Federal, State, and local officials work together to develop site-specific emergency response plans for nuclear power plant accidents. These plans are tested through exercises that include protective actions for schools and nursing homes.

The plans also delineate evacuation routes, reception centers for those seeking radiological monitoring, and location of congregate care centers for temporary lodging.

State and local governments, with support from the Federal government and utilities, develop plans that include a plume emergency planning zone with a radius of 10 miles from the plant, and an ingestion planning zone within a radius of 50 miles from the plant.

Residents within the 10-mile emergency planning zone are regularly disseminated emergency information materials (via brochures, the phone book, calendars, utility bills, etc.). These materials contain educational information on radiation, instructions for evacuation and sheltering, special arrangements for the handicapped, contacts for additional information, etc. Residents should be familiar with these emergency information materials.

Radiological emergency plans call for a prompt Alert and Notification system. If needed, this prompt Alert and Notification System will be activated quickly to inform the public of any potential threat from natural or man-made events. This system uses either sirens, tone alert radios, route alerting (the "Paul Revere" method), or a combination to notify the public to tune their radios or television to an Emergency Alert System (EAS) station.

The EAS stations will provide information and emergency instructions for the public to follow. If you are alerted, tune to your local EAS station which includes radio stations, television stations, NOAA weather radio, and the cable TV system.

Special plans must be made to assist and care for persons who are medically disabled or handicapped. If you or someone you know lives within ten miles of a nuclear facility, please notify and register with your local emergency management agency. Adequate assistance will be provided during an emergency.

In the most serious case, evacuations will be recommended based on particular plant conditions rather than waiting for the situation to deteriorate and an actual release of radionuclides to occur.

Emergency Classification Levels

Preparedness for commercial nuclear power plants includes a system for notifying the public if a problem occurs at a plant. The emergency classification level of the problem is defined by these four categories:

1. Notification of an Unusual Event is the least serious of the four levels. The event poses no threat to you or to plant employees, but emergency officials are notified. No action by the public is necessary.

2. Alert is declared when an event has occurred that could reduce the plant's level of safety, but backup plant systems still work. Emergency agencies are notified and kept informed, but no action by the public is necessary.

3. Site Area Emergency is declared when an event involving major problems with the plant's safety systems has progressed to the point that a release of some radioactivity into the air or water is possible, but is not expected to exceed Environmental Protection Agency Protective Action Guidelines (PAGs) beyond the site boundary. Thus, no action by the public is necessary.

4. General Emergency is the most serious of the four classifications and is declared when an event at the plant has caused a loss of safety systems. If such an event occurs, radiation could be released that would travel beyond the site boundary. State and local authorities will take action to protect the residents living near the plant. The alert and notification system will be sounded. People in the affected areas could be advised to evacuate promptly or, in some situations, to shelter in place. When the sirens are sounded, you should listen to your radio, television, and tone alert radios for site-specific information and instructions.

If You Are Alerted

- Remember that hearing a siren or tone alert radio does not mean you should evacuate. It means you should promptly turn to an EAS station to determine whether it is only a test or an actual emergency.
- Tune to your local radio or television station for information. The warning siren could mean a nuclear power plant emergency or the sirens could be used as a warning for tornado, fire, flood, chemical spill, etc.
- Check on your neighbors.
- Do not call 911.
- Special rumor control numbers and information will be provided to the public for a nuclear power plant emergency, either during the EAS message, in the utilities' public information brochure, or both.
- In a nuclear power plant emergency, you may be advised to go indoors and, if so, to close all windows, doors, chimney dampers, and other sources of outside air, and turn off forced air heating and cooling equipment, etc.

If You Are Advised to Evacuate the Area

- Stay calm and do not rush.
- Listen to emergency information.
- Close and lock windows and doors.
- Turn off air conditioning, vents, fans, and furnace.
- Close fire place dampers.
- Take a few items with you. Gather personal items you or your family might need:
  - Flashlight and extra batteries
  - Portable, battery operated radio and extra batteries
  - First aid kit and manual
  - Emergency food and water
  - Essential medicines
  - Cash and credit cards
- Use your own transportation or make arrangements to ride with a neighbor. Public transportation should be available for those who have not made arrangements. Keep car windows and air vents closed and listen to an EAS radio station.
- Follow the evacuation routes provided. If you need a place to stay, congregate care information will be provided.

If Advised to Remain at Home

- Bring pets inside.
- Close and lock windows and doors.
- Turn off air conditioning, vents, fans, and furnace.
- Close fireplace dampers.
- Go to the basement or other underground area.
- Stay inside until authorities say it is safe.

WHEN COMING IN FROM OUTDOORS

- Shower and change clothing and shoes.
- Put items worn outdoors in a plastic bag and seal it.
- The thyroid gland is vulnerable to the uptake of radioactive iodine. If a radiological release occurs at a nuclear power plant, states may decide to provide the public with a stable iodine,

potassium iodide, which saturates the thyroid and protects it from the uptake of radioactive iodine. Such a protective action is at the option of the state, and in some cases, local government.

- Remember your neighbors who may require special assistance—infants, elderly people, and people with disabilities.

School Evacuations

If an incident involving an actual or potential radiological release occurs, consideration is given to the safety of the children. If an emergency is declared, students in the 10-mile emergency planning zone will be relocated to designated facilities in a safe area. Usually, as a precautionary measure, school children are relocated prior to the evacuation of the general public.

For Farmers and Home Gardeners

If a radiological incident occurs at the nuclear facility, periodic information concerning the safety of farm and home grown products will be provided. Information on actions you can take to protect crops and livestock is available from your agricultural extension agent.

CROPS

- Normal harvesting and processing may still be possible if time permits.
- Unharvested crops are hard to protect.
- Crops already harvested should be stored inside if possible.
- Wash and peel vegetables and fruits before use if they were not already harvested.

LIVESTOCK

Provide as much shelter as possible. Take care of milk-producing animals, providing plenty of food and water and making sure shelters are well-ventilated. Use stored feed and water, when possible.

Three Ways to Minimize Radiation Exposure

There are three factors that minimize radiation exposure to your body: time, distance, and shielding.

Time—Most radioactivity loses its strength fairly quickly. Limiting the time spent near the source of radiation reduces the amount of radiation exposure you will receive. Following an accident, local authorities will monitor any release of radiation and determine the level of protective actions and when the threat has passed.

Distance—The more distance between you and the source of the radiation, the less radiation you will receive. In the most serious nuclear power plant accident, local officials will likely call for an evacuation, thereby increasing the distance between you and the radiation.

Shielding—Like distance, the more heavy, dense materials between you and the source of the radiation, the better. This is why local officials could advise you to remain indoors if an accident occurs. In some cases, the walls in your home or workplace would be sufficient shielding to protect you for a short period of time.

What You Can Do to Stay Informed:

- Attend public information meetings. You may also want to attend post-exercise meetings that include the media and the public.
- Contact local emergency management officials, who can provide information about radioactivity, safety precautions, and state, local, industry, and federal plans.
- Ask about the hazards radiation may pose to your family, especially with respect to young children, pregnant women, and the elderly.
- Ask where nuclear power plants are located.
- Learn your community's warning systems.
- Learn emergency plans for schools, day care centers, nursing homes—anywhere family members might be.
- Be familiar with emergency information materials that are regularly disseminated to your home (via brochures, the phone book, calendars, utility bills, etc.). These materials contain educational information on radiation, instructions for evacuation and sheltering, special arrangements for the handicapped, contacts for additional information, etc.

REFERENCE #11
DISASTER: WILDLAND FIRES

The threat of wildland fires for people living near wildland areas or using recreational facilities in wilderness areas is real. Advance planning and knowing how to protect buildings in these areas can lessen the devastation of a wildland fire.

Before

- Learn and teach safe fire practices.
- Build fires away from nearby trees or bushes.
- Always have a way to extinguish the fire quickly and completely.
- Never leave a fire—even a cigarette—burning unattended.
- Obtain local building codes and weed abatement ordinances for structures built near wooded areas.
- Use fire-resistant materials when building, renovating, or retrofitting structures.
- Create a safety zone to separate the home from combustible plants.
- Stone walls can act as heat shields and deflect flames.
- Swimming pools and patios can be a safety zone.
- Check for fire hazards around the home.
- Install electrical lines underground, if possible.
- Keep all tree and shrub limbs trimmed so they don't come in contact with wires.
- Prune all branches around the residence to a height of 8 to 10 feet.
- Keep trees adjacent to buildings free of dead or dying wood and moss.
- Remove all dead limbs, needles, and debris from rain gutters.
- Store combustible or flammable materials in approved safety containers and keep them away from the house.
- Keep chimney clean.
- Avoid open burning completely, and especially during the dry season.
- Install smoke detectors on every level of your home and near sleeping areas.

- Make evacuation plans from home and from neighborhood. Plan several routes in case the fire blocks escape route.
- Have disaster supplies on hand:
  - Flashlight with extra batteries
  - Portable, battery-operated radio and extra batteries
  - First aid kit and manual
  - Emergency food and water
  - Nonelectric can opener
  - Essential medicines
  - Cash and credit cards
  - Sturdy shoes
- Develop an emergency communication plan.
- In case family members are separated from one another during a wildland fire (a real possibility during the day when adults are at work and children are at school), have a plan for getting back together.
- Ask an out-of-state relative or friend to serve as the "family contact." After a disaster, it's often easier to call long distance. Make sure everyone knows the name, address, and phone number of the contact person.
- Contact your local emergency management office or American Red Cross chapter for more information on wildland fires.

FIRE-RESISTANT BUILDING MATERIALS

- Avoid using wooden shakes and shingles for a roof.
- Use tile, stucco, metal siding, brick, concrete block, rock, or other fire-resistant materials.
- Use only thick, tempered safety glass in large windows and sliding glass doors.

MITIGATION

Mitigation includes any activities that prevent an emergency, reduce the chance of an emergency happening, or lessen the damaging effects of unavoidable emergencies. Investing in preventive mitigation steps now such as installing a spark arrestor on your chimney, cleaning roof surfaces and gutters regularly, and using only fire resistant materials on the exterior of your home, will help reduce the impact of wildland fires in the future. For more information on mitigation, contact your local emergency management office.

During

- Turn on a battery-operated radio to get the latest emergency information.
- Remove combustible items from around the house:
  - Lawn and poolside furniture
  - Umbrellas
  - Tarp coverings
  - Firewood
- Take down flammable drapes and curtains and close all venetian blinds or noncombustible window coverings.
- Take action to protect your home.
- Close all doors and windows inside your home to prevent draft.
- Close gas valves and turn off all pilot lights.
- Turn on a light in each room for visibility in heavy smoke.
- Place valuables that will not be damaged by water in a pool or pond.
- If hoses and adequate water are available, leave sprinklers on roofs and anything that might be damaged by fire.
- Be ready to evacuate all family members and pets when fire nears or when instructed to do so by local officials.

IF TRAPPED IN A WILDLAND FIRE

- You cannot outrun a fire.
- Crouch in a pond or river.
- Cover head and upper body with wet clothing.
- If water is not around, look for shelter in a cleared area or among a bed of rocks. Lie flat and cover body with wet clothing or soil.
- Breathe the air close to the ground through a wet cloth to avoid scorching lungs or inhaling smoke.

After

- Take care when re-entering a burned wildland area. Hot spots can flare up without warning.
- Check the roof immediately and extinguish any sparks or embers.
- Check the attic for hidden burning sparks. For several hours afterward, re-check for smoke and sparks throughout the home.

REFERENCE #12
DISASTER: TERRORISM

A terrorist attack with conventional weapons such as firearms, explosives, or incendiary devices in the United States remains possible, though unlikely.

Before

- Learn about the nature of terrorism.
- Terrorists often choose targets that offer little danger to themselves and areas with relatively easy public access.
- Foreign terrorists look for visible targets where they can avoid detection before or after an attack such as international airports, large cities, major international events, resorts, and high-profile landmarks.
- Learn about the different types of terrorist weapons including explosives, kidnappings, hijackings, arson, and shootings.
- Prepare to deal with a terrorist incident by adapting many of the same techniques used to prepare for other crises.
- Be alert and aware of the surrounding area. The very nature of terrorism suggests that there may be little or no warning.
- Take precautions when traveling. Be aware of conspicuous or unusual behavior. Do not accept packages from strangers. Do not leave luggage unattended.
- Learn where emergency exists are located.
- Think ahead about how to evacuate a building, subway, or congested public area in a hurry.
- Learn where staircases are located.
- Notice your immediate surroundings. Be aware of heavy or breakable objects that could move, fall, or break in an explosion.

PREPARING FOR A BUILDING EXPLOSION

The use of explosives by terrorists can result in collapsed buildings and fires. People who live or work in a multi-level building can do the following:

- Review emergency evacuation procedures.
- Know where fire exits are located.
- Keep fire extinguishers in working order. Know where they are located, and how to use them.
- Learn first aid.
- Contact the local chapter of the American Red Cross for additional information.
- Keep the following items in a designated place on each floor of the building:
  - Portable, battery-operated radio and extra batteries
  - Several flashlights and extra batteries
  - First aid kit and manual
  - Several hard hats
  - Fluorescent tape to rope off dangerous areas

BOMB THREATS

- If you receive a bomb threat, get as much information from the caller as possible. Keep the caller on the line and record everything that is said. Notify the police and the building management.
- After you've been notified of a bomb threat, do not touch any suspicious packages. Clear the area around the suspicious package and notify the police immediately.
- In evacuating a building, avoid standing in front of windows or other potentially hazardous areas. Do not restrict sidewalk or streets to be used by emergency officials.

During

- In a building explosion, get out of the building as quickly and calmly as possible.
- If items are falling off of bookshelves or from the ceiling, get under a sturdy table or desk.
- If there is a fire:
  - Stay low to the floor and exit the building as quickly as possible.
  - Cover nose and mouth with a wet cloth.
  - When approaching a closed door, use the palm of your hand and forearm to feel the lower, middle, and upper parts of the

door. If it is not hot, brace yourself against the door and open
it slowly. If it is hot to the touch, do not open the door—seek
an alternate escape route.

- Heavy smoke and poisonous gases collect first along the ceiling. Stay below the smoke at all times.

After

IF YOU ARE TRAPPED IN DEBRIS:

- Use a flashlight.
- Stay in your area so that you don't kick up dust. Cover your mouth with a handkerchief or clothing.
- Tap on a pipe or wall so that rescuers can hear where you are. Use a whistle if one is available. Shout only as a last resort—shouting can cause a person to inhale dangerous amounts of dust.

ASSISTING VICTIMS

- Untrained persons should not attempt to rescue people who are inside a collapsed building. Wait for emergency personnel to arrive.

Chemical Agents

- Chemical agents are poisonous gases, liquids, or solids that have toxic effects on people, animals, or plants. Most chemical agents cause serious injuries or death.
- Severity of injuries depends on the type and amount of the chemical agent used, and the duration of exposure.
- Were a chemical agent attack to occur, authorities would instruct citizens to either seek shelter where they are and seal the premises or evacuate immediately.
- Exposure to chemical agents can be fatal.
- Leaving the shelter to rescue or assist victims can be a deadly decision. There is no assistance that the untrained can offer that would likely be of any value to the victims of chemical agents.

Biological Agents

Biological agents are organisms or toxins that have illness-producing effects on people, livestock, and crops.

Because biological agents cannot necessarily be detected and may take time to grow and cause a disease, it is almost impossible to know that a biological attack has occurred. If government officials become aware of a biological attack through an informant or warning by terrorists, they would most likely instruct citizens to either seek shelter where they are and seal the premises or evacuate immediately.

A person affected by a biological agent requires the immediate attention of professional medical personnel. Some agents are contagious, and victims may need to be quarantined. Also, some medical facilities may not receive victims for fear of contaminating the hospital population.

REFERENCE #13
DISASTER: HAZARDOUS MATERIALS ACCIDENTS

A hazardous materials accident can occur anywhere. Communities located near chemical manufacturing plants are particularly at risk. However, hazardous materials are transported on our roadways, railways, and waterways daily, so any area is considered vulnerable to an accident.

Before

- Learn to detect the presence of a hazardous material.
- Many hazardous materials do not have a taste or an odor. Some materials can be detected because they cause physical reactions such as watering eyes or nausea. Some hazardous materials exist beneath the surface of the ground and can be recognized by an oil or foam-like appearance.
- Contact your Local Emergency Planning Committee (LEPC) or local emergency management office for information about hazardous materials and community response plans.
- Find out evacuation plans for your workplace and your children's schools.
- Be ready to evacuate. Plan several evacuation routes out of the area.
- Ask about industry and community warning systems.
- Have disaster supplies on hand:
  - Flashlight and extra batteries
  - Portable, battery-operated radio and extra batteries
  - First aid kit and manual
  - Emergency food and water
  - Nonelectric can opener
  - Essential medicines
  - Cash and credit cards
  - Sturdy shoes
- Develop an emergency communication plan.

- In case family members are separated from one another during a hazardous materials accident (this is a real possibility during the day when adults are at work and children are at school), develop a plan for reuniting after the disaster.
- Ask an out-of-state relative or friend to serve as the "family contact." After a disaster, it's often easier to call long distance. Make sure everyone knows the name, address, and phone number of the contact person.

During

If you hear a siren or other warning signal, turn on a radio or television for further emergency information.

IF CAUGHT AT THE SCENE OF AN ACCIDENT

- If you see an accident, call 9-1-1 or the local fire department to report the nature and location of the accident as soon as possible.
- Move away from the accident scene and help keep others away.
- Do not walk into or touch any of the spilled substance. Try not to inhale gases, fumes, and smoke. If possible, cover mouth with a cloth while leaving the area.
- Stay away from accident victims until the hazardous material has been identified.
- Try to stay upstream, uphill, and upwind of the accident.

IF ASKED TO STAY INDOORS ("IN-PLACE SHELTERING")

- Seal house so contaminants cannot enter.
- Close and lock windows and doors.
- Seal gaps under doorways and windows with wet towels and duct tape.
- Seal gaps around window and air conditioning units, bathroom and kitchen exhaust fans, and stove and dryer vents with duct tape and plastic sheeting, waxed paper, or aluminum wrap.
- Close fireplace dampers.
- Close off nonessential rooms such as storage areas, laundry rooms, and extra bedrooms.

- Turn off ventilation systems.
- Don't try to care for victims of a hazardous materials accident until the substance has been identified and authorities indicate it is safe to go near victims. Then you can move victims to fresh air and call for emergency medical care.
- Cleanse victims that have come in contact with chemicals by immediately pouring cold water over the skin or eyes for at least 15 minutes, unless authorities instruct you not to use water on the particular chemical involved.
- Remove contaminated clothing and shoes and place them in a plastic bag.
- Bring pets inside.
- Immediately after the "in-place sheltering" announcement is issued, fill up bathtubs or large containers for an additional water supply and turn off the intake valve to the house.
- If gas or vapors could have entered the building, take shallow breaths through a cloth or a towel.
- Avoid eating or drinking any food or water that may be contaminated.
- Monitor the Emergency Broadcast System station for further updates and remain in shelter until authorities indicate it is safe to come out.

EVACUATION

Authorities will decide if evacuation is necessary based primarily on the type and amount of chemical released and how long it is expected to affect an area. Other considerations are the length of time it should take to evacuate the area, weather conditions, and the time of day.

IF ASKED TO EVACUATE

- Stay tuned to a radio or television for information on evacuation routes, temporary shelters, and procedures.
- Follow the routes recommended by the authorities—shortcuts may not be safe. Leave at once.
- If you have time, minimize contamination in the house by closing all windows, shutting all vents, and turning off attic fans.

- Take preassembled disaster supplies.
- Remember to help your neighbors who may require special assistance—infants, elderly people, and people with disabilities.

After

- Return home only when authorities say it is safe.
- Follow local instructions concerning the safety of food and water.
- Clean up and dispose of residue carefully. Follow instructions from emergency officials concerning clean-up methods.

REFERENCE #14
DISASTER: LANDSLIDES AND MUD FLOWS

Landslide and mud flows usually strike without warning. The force of rocks, soil, or other debris moving down a slope can devastate anything in its path. Take the following steps to be ready.

Before

- Get a ground assessment of your property.
- Your county geologist or county planning department may have specific information on areas vulnerable to landsliding. Consult a professional geotechnical expert for opinions and advice on landslide problems and on corrective measures you can take.

MINIMIZE HOME HAZARDS

- Plant ground cover on slopes and build retaining walls.
- In mud flow areas, build channels or deflection walls to direct the flow around buildings.
- Remember: If you build walls to divert debris flow and the flow lands on a neighbor's property, you may be liable for damages.

LEARN TO RECOGNIZE THE LANDSLIDE WARNING SIGNS

- Doors or windows stick or jam for the first time.
- New cracks appear in plaster, tile, brick, or foundations.
- Outside walls, walks, or stairs begin pulling away from the building.
- Slowly developing, widening cracks appear on the ground or on paved areas such as streets or driveways.
- Underground utility lines break.
- Bulging ground appears at the base of a slope.
- Water breaks through the ground surface in new locations.
- Fences, retaining walls, utility poles, or trees tilt or move.
- You hear a faint rumbling sound that increases in volume as the landslide nears.
- The ground slopes downward in one specific direction and may begin shifting in that direction under your feet.

MAKE EVACUATION PLANS

- Plan at least two evacuation routes since roads may become blocked or closed.
- Develop an emergency communication plan.
- In case family members are separated from one another during a landslide or mud flow (this is a real possibility during the day when adults are at work and children are at school), have a plan for getting back together.
- Ask an out-of-state relative or friend to serve as the "family contact." After a disaster, it's often easier to call long distance. Make sure everyone knows the name, address, and phone number of the contact person.

INSURANCE

Mud flow is covered by flood insurance policies from the National Flood Insurance Program. Flood insurance can be purchased through a local insurance agency.

MITIGATION

Mitigation includes any activities that prevent an emergency, reduce the chance of an emergency happening, or lessen the damaging effects of unavoidable emergencies. Investing in preventive mitigation steps now such as planting ground cover (low growing plants) on slopes, or installing flexible pipe fitting to avoid gas or water leaks, will help reduce the impact of landslides and mud flows in the future. For more information on mitigation, contact your local emergency management office.

During

IF INSIDE A BUILDING:

- Stay inside.
- Take cover under a desk, table, or other piece of sturdy furniture.

IF OUTDOORS:

- Try to get out of the path of the landslide or mud flow.
- Run to the nearest high ground in a direction away from the path.
- If rocks and other debris are approaching, run for the nearest shelter such as a group of trees or a building.
- If escape is not possible, curl into a tight ball and protect your head.

SINKHOLES

A sinkhole occurs when groundwater dissolves a vulnerable land surface such as limestone, causing the land surface to collapse from a lack of support. In June 1993, a 100-foot wide, 25-foot deep sinkhole formed under a hotel parking lot in Atlanta, killing two people and engulfing numerous cars.

After

- Stay away from the slide area. There may be danger of additional slides.
- Check for injured and trapped persons near the slide area. Give first aid if trained.
- Remember to help your neighbors who may require special assistance—infants, elderly people, and people with disabilities.
- Listen to a battery-operated radio or television for the latest emergency information.
- Remember that flooding may occur after a mud flow or a landslide.
- Check for damaged utility lines. Report any damage to the utility company.
- Check the building foundation, chimney, and surrounding land for damage.
- Replant damaged ground as soon as possible since erosion caused by loss of ground cover can lead to flash flooding.
- Seek the advice of geotechnical expert for evaluating landslide hazards or designing corrective techniques to reduce landslide risk.

REFERENCE #15
DISASTER: VOLCANOES

Volcanic eruptions can hurl hot rocks for at least 20 miles. Floods, airborne ash, or noxious fumes can spread 100 miles or more. If you live near a known volcano, active or dormant, be ready to evacuate at a moment's notice.

Before

- Learn about your community warning systems.
- Be prepared for these disasters that can be spawned by volcanoes.
  - Earthquakes
  - Flash floods
  - Landslides and mud flows
  - Thunderstorms
  - Tsunamis
- Make evacuation plans. You want to get to high ground away from the eruption. Plan a route out and have a backup route in mind.
- Develop an emergency communication plan.
- In case family members are separated from one another during a volcanic eruption (a real possibility during the day when adults are at work and children are at school), have a plan for getting back together.
- Ask an out-of-state relative or friend to serve as the "family contact." After a disaster, it's often easier to call long distance. Make sure everyone knows the name, address, and phone number of the contact person.
- Have disaster supplies on hand.
  - Flashlight and extra batteries
  - Portable, battery-operated radio and extra batteries
  - First aid kit and manual
  - Emergency food and water
  - Nonelectric can opener
  - Essential medicines
  - Cash and credit cards
  - Sturdy shoes

- Get a pair of goggles and a throw-away breathing mask for each member of the household.
- Contact your local emergency management office or American Red Cross chapter for more information on volcanoes.

EVACUATION

Although it may seem safe to stay at home and wait out an eruption, doing so could be very dangerous. The rock debris from a volcano can break windows and set buildings on fire. Stay safe. Follow authorities' instructions and leave the area before the disaster begins.

During

- Follow the evacuation order issued by authorities.
- Avoid areas downwind of the volcano.

IF CAUGHT INDOORS:

- Close all windows, doors, and dampers.
- Put all machinery inside a garage or barn.
- Bring animals and livestock into closed shelters.

IF OUTDOORS:

- Seek shelter indoors.
- If caught in a rockfall, roll into a ball to protect head.
- Avoid low-lying areas where poisonous gases can collect and flash floods can be most dangerous.
- If caught near a stream, beware of mud flows.

PROTECT YOURSELF:

- Wear long-sleeved shirts and long pants.
- Use goggles to protect eyes.
- Use masks for breathing.
- Keep car or truck engines off.
- Stay out of the area.

- A lateral blast of a volcano can travel many miles from the mountain. Trying to watch an erupting volcano is a deadly idea.

MUD FLOWS

Mud flows are powerful "rivers" of mud that can move faster than people can walk or run. Mud flows occur when rain falls through ash-carrying clouds or when rivers are dammed during an eruption. They are most dangerous close to stream channels.

When you approach a bridge, first look upstream. If a mud flow is approaching or moving beneath the bridge, do not cross the bridge. The power of the mud flow can destroy a bridge very quickly.

After

- Listen to a battery-powered radio or television for the latest emergency information.
- Stay away from volcanic ashfall.

WHEN OUTSIDE:

- Cover your mouth and nose. A number of victims of the Mount St. Helens volcano died from inhaling ash.
- Wear goggles to protect your eyes.
- Keep skin covered to avoid irritation or burns.
- If you have a respiratory ailment, avoid contact with any amount of ash.
- Stay indoors until local health officials advise it is safe to go outside.
- Avoid driving in heavy ashfall. Driving will stir up more ash that can clog engines and stall vehicles.
- Clear roofs of ashfall. Ashfall is very heavy and can cause buildings to collapse.
- Remember to help your neighbors who may require special assistance—infants, elderly people, and people with disabilities.

REFERENCE #16
DISASTER: EXTREME HEAT

Doing too much on a hot day, spending too much time in the sun or staying too long in an overheated place can cause heat-related illnesses. Know the symptoms of heat disorders and overexposure to the sun, and be ready to give first aid treatment.

Before

- Contact your local emergency management office or American Red Cross chapter for information on extreme heat.
- Install window air conditioners snugly.
- Close any floor heat registers nearby.
- Insulate spaces around air conditioners for a tighter fit.
- Use a circulating or box fan to spread the cool air.
- Keep heat outside and cool air inside.
- Install temporary reflectors, such as aluminum foil covered cardboard, to reflect any heat back outside. Keep the cool air inside by weather-stripping doors and windowsills.
- Consider keeping storm windows up all year. Storm windows can keep the heat out of a house in the summer the same way they keep the cold out in the winter. Check air-conditioning ducts for proper insulation.

During

- Protect windows. Hang shades, draperies, awnings, or louvers on windows that receive morning or afternoon sun. Outdoor awnings or louvers can reduce the heat entering the house by as much as 80%.
- Conserve electricity. During periods of extreme heat, people tend to use a lot more power for air conditioning, which can lead to a power shortage or outage. Stay indoors as much as possible. If air conditioning is not available, stay on the lowest floor out of the sunshine. Remember that electric fans do not cool, they just blow hot air around.
- Eat well-balanced, light meals.

- Drink plenty of water regularly.
- Persons who have epilepsy or heart, kidney, or liver disease; are on fluid-restrictive diets; or have a problem with fluid retention should consult a doctor before increasing liquid intake.
- Limit intake of alcoholic beverages. Although beer and alcoholic beverages appear to satisfy thirst, they actually cause further body dehydration.
- Dress in loose-fitting clothes that cover as much skin as possible. Lightweight, light-colored clothing reflects heat and sunlight and helps maintain normal body temperature.
- Protect face and head by wearing a wide-brimmed hat.
- Allow your body to get acclimated to hot temperatures for the first 2 or 3 days of a heat wave.
- Avoid too much sunshine. Sunburn slows the skin's ability to cool itself. Use a sunscreen lotion with a high SPF (sun protection factor) rating.
- Avoid extreme temperature changes. A cool shower immediately after coming in from hot temperatures can result in hypothermia, particularly for elderly and very young people.
- Slow down. Reduce, eliminate, or reschedule strenuous activities. High-risk individuals should stay in cool places.
- Get plenty of rest to allow your natural "cooling system" to work. Take salt tablets only if specified by your physician. Persons on salt-restrictive diets should check with a physician before increasing salt intake.
- Vacuum air conditioner filters weekly during periods of high use.
- Learn the symptoms of heat disorders and know how to give first aid.

During a Drought

Lower water use. Watering the lawn and washing the car is water that could be used to drink and flush. Farmers should contact the county Farm Service Agency for disaster assistance information.

Heat Disorders

SUNBURN

Symptoms:
Skin redness and pain, possible swelling, blisters, fever, headaches.

First Aid:
Take a shower, using soap, to remove oils that may block pores preventing the body from cooling naturally.

If blisters occur, apply dry, sterile dressings and get medical attention.

HEAT CRAMPS

Symptoms:
Painful spasms usually in leg and abdominal muscles. Heavy sweating.

First Aid:
Firm pressure on cramping muscles or gentle massage to relieve spasm. Give sips of water. If nausea occurs, discontinue.

HEAT EXHAUSTION

Symptoms:
Heavy sweating, weakness. Skin cold, pale, and clammy. Weak pulse. Normal temperature possible. Fainting, vomiting.

First Aid:
Get victim to lie down in a cool place. Loosen clothing. Apply cool, wet cloths. Fan or move victim to air-conditioned place. Give sips of water. If nausea occurs, discontinue. If vomiting occurs, seek immediate medical attention.

HEAT STROKE (SUN STROKE)

Symptoms:
High body temperature (106+). Hot, dry skin. Rapid, strong pulse. Possible unconsciousness. Victim will likely not sweat.

First Aid:
Heat stroke is a severe medical emergency. Call 9-1-1 or emergency medical services or get the victim to a hospital immediately. Delay

can be fatal. Move victim to a cooler environment. Try a cool bath or sponging to reduce body temperature. Use extreme caution. Remove clothing. Use fans and/or air conditioners. DO NOT GIVE FLUIDS.

REFERENCE #17
DISASTER: TSUNAMIS

A tsunami is a series of waves that may be dangerous and destructive. When you hear a tsunami warning, move at once to higher ground and stay there until local authorities say it is safe to return home.

Before

- Find out if your home is in a danger area.
- Know the height of your street above sea level and the distance of your street from the coast. Evacuation orders may be based on these numbers.
- Be familiar with the tsunami warning signs. Because tsunamis can be caused by an underwater disturbance or an earthquake, people living along the coast should consider an earthquake or a sizable ground rumbling as a warning signal. A noticeable rapid rise or fall in coastal waters is also a sign that a tsunami is approaching.
- Make sure all family members know how to respond to a tsunami.
- Make evacuation plans. Pick an inland location that is elevated. After an earthquake or other natural disaster, roads in and out of the vicinity may be blocked, so pick more than one evacuation route.
- Teach family members how and when to turn off gas, electricity, and water.
- Teach children how and when to call 9-1-1, police or fire department, and which radio station to listen for official information.
- Have disaster supplies on hand:
  - Flashlight and extra batteries
  - Portable, battery-operated radio and extra batteries
  - First aid kit and manual
  - Emergency food and water
  - Nonelectric can opener
  - Essential medicines
  - Cash and credit cards
  - Sturdy shoes
- Develop an emergency communication plan.

- In case family members are separated from one another during a tsunami (a real possibility during the day when adults are at work and children are at school), have a plan for getting back together.
- Ask an out-of-state relative or friend to serve as the "family contact." After a disaster, often it's easier to call long distance. Make sure everyone knows the name, address, and phone number of the contact person.
- Contact your local emergency management office or American Red Cross chapter for more information on tsunamis.

During

- Listen to a radio or television to get the latest emergency information, and be ready to evacuate if asked to do so.
- If you hear an official tsunami warning or detect signs of a tsunami, evacuate at once. Climb to higher ground. A tsunami warning is issued when authorities are certain that a tsunami threat exists.
- Stay away from the beach.
- Never go down to the beach to watch a tsunami come in. If you can see the wave you are too close to escape it.
- Return home only after authorities advise it is safe to do so.
- A tsunami is a series of waves. Do not assume that one wave means that the danger over. The next wave may be larger than the first one. Stay out of the area.

After

- Stay tuned to a battery-operated radio for the latest emergency information.
- Help injured or trapped persons.
- Give first aid where appropriate. Do not move seriously injured persons unless they are in immediate danger of further injury. Call for help.
- Remember to help your neighbors who may require special assistance—infants, elderly people, and people with disabilities.
- Stay out of damaged buildings. Return home only when authorities say it is safe.

- Enter your home with caution. Use a flashlight when entering damaged buildings. Check for electrical shorts and live wires. Do not use appliances or lights until an electrician has checked the electrical system.
- Open windows and doors to help dry the building.
- Shovel mud while it is still moist to give walls and floors an opportunity to dry.
- Check food supplies and test drinking water.
- Fresh food that has come in contact with flood waters may be contaminated and should be thrown out. Have tap water tested by the local health department.

INSPECTING UTILITIES IN A DAMAGED HOME

- Check for gas leaks—If you smell gas or hear a blowing or hissing noise, open a window and quickly leave the building. Turn off the gas at the outside main valve if you can and call the gas company from a neighbor's home. If you turn off the gas for any reason, it must be turned back on by a professional.
- Look for electrical system damage—If you see sparks or broken or frayed wires, or if you smell hot insulation, turn off the electricity at the main fuse box or circuit breaker. If you have to step in water to get to the fuse box or circuit breaker, call an electrician first for advice.
- Check for sewage and water lines damage—If you suspect sewage lines are damaged, avoid using toilets and call a plumber. If water pipes are damaged, contact the water company and avoid the water from the tap. You can obtain safe water by melting ice cubes.

REFERENCE #18
FIRE SAFETY DURING AND
AFTER A DISASTER

(From FEMA-Federal Emergency Management Agency)

A wide range of natural disasters occur within the United States every year. Natural disasters can have a devastating effect on you and your home. The Federal Emergency Management Agency's U.S. Fire Administration encourages you to use the following safety tips to help protect yourself, your family, and your home from the potential threat of fire during or after a disaster. You can greatly reduce your chances of becoming a fire casualty by being able to identify potential hazards and following the outlined safety tips.

Facts on Fire: Fire in the United States

The U.S. has one of the highest fire death rates in the industrialized world. About 5,000 people die every year in this country as the result of fire, and another 25,500 are injured.

About 100 firefighters are killed annually in duty-related incidents. Each year, fire kills more Americans than all natural disasters combined. Fire is the third leading cause of accidental death in the home; at least 80% of all fire deaths occur in residences. More than 2 million fires are reported each year. Many others go unreported, causing additional injuries and property loss. Direct property loss due to fires is estimated at $9.4 billion annually.

Causes of Fires and Fire Deaths

Cooking is the leading cause of home fires in the U.S. It is also the leading cause of fire injuries. Cooking fires often result from unattended cooking and human error, rather than mechanical failure of stoves or ovens. Careless smoking is the leading cause of fire deaths. Smoke detectors and smolder-resistant bedding and upholstered furniture are significant fire deterrents. Heating is the second leading cause of residential fires and ties with arson as the second leading cause of fire deaths. However, heating fires are a larger problem in single family homes than in apartments. Unlike apartments, the heating systems in single family homes are often not professionally maintained. Arson is the third leading cause of residential fires and a leading cause of residential fire deaths. In commercial properties, arson is the major cause of deaths, injuries, and dollar loss.

Who is most at risk

Senior citizens and children under the age of five have the greatest risk of fire death. The fire death risk among seniors is more than double the average population. The fire death risk for children under age five is nearly double the risk of the average population. Children under the age of ten accounted for an estimated 20% of all fire deaths in 1995. Over 30% of the fires that kill young children are started by children playing with fire. Men die or are injured in fires twice as often as women.

What Saves Lives

A working smoke alarm dramatically increases a person's chance of surviving a fire. Approximately 90% of U.S. homes have at least one smoke alarm. However, these alarms are not always properly maintained and as a result might not work in an emergency.

There has been a disturbing increase over the last ten years in the number of fires that occur in homes with non-functioning alarms. It is estimated that over 40% of residential fires and three-fifths of residential fatalities occur in homes with no smoke alarms. Residential sprinklers have become more cost effective for homes. Currently, few homes are protected by them.

Earthquakes

SOME TYPES OF FIRE RELATED HAZARDS PRESENT DURING AND AFTER AN EARTHQUAKE

Appliances, furniture, and household products can shift, fall, and spill. Gas, chemical, and electrical hazards may be present. Leaking gas lines, damaged or leaking gas propane containers, and leaking vehicle gas tanks could explode or ignite. Pools of water or even appliances can be electrically charged.

CHEMICAL SAFETY.   Look for flammable liquids like gasoline, lighter fluid, and paint thinner that may have spilled.Thoroughly clean the spill and place containers in a well-ventilated area. Keep combustible liquids away from heat sources.

ELECTRICAL SAFETY.   If you can safely get to the main breaker or fuse box, turn off the power. Look for items that might have jarred loose during the earthquake. Appliances or power connectors could create a fire hazard. Assume all wires on the ground are electrically charged. This includes cable TV feeds. Look for and replace frayed or cracked extension and appliance cords, loose prongs, and plugs. Exposed outlets and wiring could present a fire and life safety hazard. Appliances that emit smoke or sparks should be repaired or replaced. Have a licensed electrician check your home for damage.

GAS SAFETY.   Smell and listen for leaky gas connections. If you believe there is a gas leak, immediately leave the house and leave the door(s) open. Never strike a match. Any size flame can spark an explosion. Before turning the gas back on, have the gas system checked by a professional.

GENERATOR SAFETY.   Follow the manufacturer's instructions and guidelines when using generators. Use a generator or other fuel-powered machines outside the home. Carbon monoxide fumes are odorless and can quickly overwhelm you indoors. Use the appropriate size and type of power cords to carry the electric load. Overloaded cords can overheat and cause fires. Never run cords under rugs or carpets where heat might build up or damage to a cord may go unnoticed. Never connect generators to another power source such as power lines. The reverse flow of electricity or "backfeed" can electrocute an unsuspecting utility worker.

HEATING SAFETY.   Kerosene heaters may not be legal in your area and should only be used where approved by authorities. Do not use the kitchen oven range to heat your home. In addition to being a fire hazard, it can be a source of toxic fumes. Alternative heaters need their space. Keep anything combustible at least 3 feet away. Make sure your alternative heaters have "tip switches." These "tip switches" are designed to automatically turn off the heater in the event they tip over. Only use the type of fuel recommended by the manufacturer and follow suggested guidelines. Never refill a space heater while it is operating or still hot. Refuel heaters only outdoors.

Make sure wood stoves are properly installed, and at least 3 feet away from combustible materials. Ensure that they have the proper floor support and adequate ventilation. Use a glass or metal screen in front of your fireplace to prevent sparks from igniting nearby carpets, furniture, or other combustible items.

AND REMEMBER...

Be careful when using candles. Keep the flame away from combustible objects and out of the reach of children. Some smoke alarms may be dependent on your home's electrical service and could be inoperative during a power outage. Check to see if your smoke alarm uses a back-up battery and install a new battery at least once a year. Smoke alarms should be installed on every level of your home. All smoke alarms should be tested monthly. All batteries should be replaced with new ones at least once a year. If there is a fire hydrant near your home, keep it clear of debris for easy access by the fire department.

Tornado or Hurricane

SOME TYPES OF FIRE RELATED HAZARDS PRESENT DURING AND AFTER A TORNADO OR HURRICANE

Leaking gas lines, damaged or leaking gas propane containers, and leaking vehicle gas tanks may explode or ignite. Debris can easily ignite, especially if electrical wires are severed. Pools of water and even appliances can be electrically charged. Generators are often used during power outages. Generators that are not properly used and maintained can be very hazardous. Alternative heating devices used incorrectly create fire hazards. Proper use and maintenance can decrease the possibility of a fire. Appliances that emit smoke or sparks should be repaired or replaced.

CHEMICAL SAFETY.   Look for combustible liquids like gasoline, lighter fluid, and paint thinner that may have spilled. Thoroughly clean the spill and place containers in a well-ventilated area. Keep combustible liquids away from heat sources.

ELECTRICAL SAFETY.   Assume all wires on the ground are electrically charged. This includes cable TV feeds. Look for and replace frayed or cracked extension and appliance cords, loose prongs, and plugs. Exposed outlets and wiring could present a fire and life safety hazard. Appliances that emit smoke or sparks should be repaired or replaced. Have a licensed electrician check your home for damage.

GAS SAFETY.   Smell and listen for leaky gas connections. If you believe there is a gas leak, immediately leave the house and leave the door(s) open. Never strike a match. Any size flame can spark an explosion. Before turning the gas back on, have the gas system checked by a professional.

GENERATOR SAFETY.   Follow the manufacturer's instructions and guidelines when using generators. Use a generator or other fuel-powered machines outside the home. Carbon monoxide fumes are odorless and can quickly overwhelm you indoors. Use the appropriate size and type of power cords to carry the electric load. Overloaded cords can overheat and cause fires. Never run cords under rugs or carpets where heat might build up or damage to a cord may go unnoticed. Never connect generators to another power source such as power lines. The reverse flow of electricity or "backfeed" can electrocute an unsuspecting utility worker.

HEATING SAFETY.   Kerosene heaters may not be legal in your area and should only be used where approved by authorities. Do not use the kitchen oven range to heat your home. In addition to being a fire hazard, it can be a source of toxic fumes. Alternative heaters need their space. Keep anything combustible at least 3 feet away. Make sure your alternative heaters have "tip switches." These "tip switches" are designed to automatically turn off the heater in the event they tip over. Only use the type of fuel recommended by the manufacturer and follow suggested guidelines. Never refill a space heater while it is operating or still hot. Refuel heaters only outdoors.

Make sure wood stoves are properly installed, and at least 3 feet away from combustible materials. Ensure they have the proper floor support and adequate ventilation. Use a glass or metal screen in front of your fireplace to prevent sparks from igniting nearby carpets, furniture, or other combustible items.

AND REMEMBER...

Be careful when using candles. Keep the flame away from combustible objects and out of the reach of children. Some smoke alarms may be dependent on your home's electrical service and could be inoperative during a power outage. Check to see if your smoke alarm uses a back-up battery and install a new battery at least once a year. Smoke alarms should be installed on every level of your home. All smoke alarms should be tested monthly. All batteries should be replaced with new ones at least once a year. If there is a fire hydrant near your home, keep it clear of debris for easy access by the fire department.

Floods

TYPES OF FIRE RELATED HAZARDS PRESENT DURING AND AFTER A FLOOD

Generators are often used during power outages. Unless generators are properly used and maintained, they can be very hazardous. Alternative heating devices used incorrectly create fire hazards. Proper use and maintenance can decrease the possibility of a fire. Leaking above ground gas lines, damaged or leaking gas or propane containers, and leaking vehicle gas tanks may explode or ignite. Pools of water and even appliances can be electrically charged. This can result in a dangerous electrical fire. Appliances that have been exposed to water can short and become a fire hazard.

CHEMICAL SAFETY.   Look for combustible liquids like gasoline, lighter fluid, and paint thinner that may have spilled. Thoroughly clean the spill and place containers in a well-ventilated area. Keep combustible liquids away from heat sources.

ELECTRICAL SAFETY.   If your home has sustained flood or water damage, and you can safely get to the main breaker or fuse box, turn off the power. Assume all wires on the ground are electrically charged. This includes cable TV feeds. Be aware of and avoid downed utility lines. Report downed or damaged power lines to the utility company or emergency services. Remove standing water, wet carpets, and furnishings. Air dry your home with good ventilation before restoring power. Have a licensed electrician check your home for damage.

GENERATOR SAFETY.   Follow the manufacturer's instructions and guidelines when using generators. Use a generator or other fuel-powered machines outside the home. Carbon monoxide fumes are odorless and can quickly overwhelm you indoors. Use the appropriate size and type of power cords to carry the electric load. Overloaded cords can overheat and cause fires. Never run cords under rugs or carpets where heat might build up or damage to a cord may go unnoticed. Always refuel generators outdoors. Never connect generators to another power source such as power lines. The reverse flow of electricity or "backfeed" can electrocute an unsuspecting utility worker.

HEATING SAFETY.   Kerosene heaters may not be legal in your area and should only be used where approved by authorities. Do not use the kitchen oven range to heat your home. In addition to being a fire hazard, it can be a source of toxic fumes. Alternative heaters need their space. Keep anything combustible at least 3 feet away. Make sure your alternative heaters have "tip switches." These "tip switches" are designed to automatically turn off the heater in the event they tip over. Only use the type of fuel recommended by the manufacturer and follow suggested guidelines.

Never refill a space heater while it is operating or still hot. Refuel heaters only outdoors. Make sure wood stoves are properly installed, and at least 3 feet away from combustible materials. Ensure that they have the proper floor support and adequate ventilation. Use a glass or metal screen in front of your fireplace to prevent sparks from igniting nearby carpets, furniture, or other combustible items.

AND REMEMBER...

Do not use alternative heating devices to dry clothes or furnishings. Be careful when using candles. Keep the flame away from combustible objects and out of the reach of children. Never thaw frozen pipes with a blow torch or other open flame. Use hot water or a UL listed device such as a hand held dryer. Some smoke alarms may be dependent on your home's electrical service and could be inoperative during a power outage. Check to see if your smoke alarm uses a back-up battery and install a new battery at least once a year. Smoke alarms should be installed on every level of your home. All smoke alarms should be tested monthly. All batteries should be replaced with new ones at least once a year. If there is a fire hydrant near your home, keep it clear of debris for easy access by the fire department.

Winter Storms

SOME TYPES OF FIRE RELATED HAZARDS PRESENT DURING AND AFTER A WINTER STORM

Alternative heating devices used incorrectly create fire hazards. Damaged or downed utility lines can present a fire and life safety hazard. Water damaged appliances and utilities can be electrically charged. Frozen water pipes can burst and cause safety hazards. Leaking gas lines, damaged or leaking gas propane containers, and leaking vehicle gas tanks may explode or ignite. Generators are often used during power outages. Generators that are not properly used and maintained can be very hazardous.

CHEMICAL SAFETY. Look for combustible liquids like gasoline, lighter fluid, and paint thinner that may have spilled. Thoroughly clean the spill and place containers in a well-ventilated area. Keep combustible liquids away from heat sources.

ELECTRICAL SAFETY. If your home has sustained flood or water damage, and you can safely get to the main breaker or fuse box, turn off the power. Assume all wires on the ground are electrically charged. This includes cable TV feeds. Look for and replace frayed or cracked extension and appliance cords, loose prongs, and plugs. Exposed outlets and wiring could present a fire and life safety hazard. Appliances that emit smoke or sparks should be repaired or replaced. Have a licensed electrician check your home for damage.

GAS SAFETY. Smell and listen for leaky gas connections. If you believe there is a gas leak, immediately leave the house and leave the door(s) open. Never strike a match. Any size flame can spark an explosion. Before turning the gas back on, have the gas system checked by a professional.

GENERATOR SAFETY. Follow the manufacturer's instructions and guidelines when using generators. Use a generator or other fuel-powered machines outside the home. Carbon monoxide fumes are odorless and can quickly overwhelm you indoors. Use the appropriate size and type of power cords to carry the electric load. Overloaded cords can overheat and cause fires. Never run cords under rugs or carpets where heat might build up or damage to a cord may go unnoticed. Never connect generators to another power source such as power lines. The reverse flow of electricity or "backfeed" can electrocute an unsuspecting utility worker.

HEATING SAFETY. Kerosene heaters may not be legal in your area and should only be used where approved by authorities. Do not use the kitchen oven range to heat your home. In addition to being a fire hazard, it can be a source of toxic fumes. Alternative heaters need their space. Keep anything combustible at least 3 feet away. Make sure your alternative heaters have "tip switches." These "tip switches" are designed to automatically turn off the heater in the event they tip over. Only use the type of fuel recommended by the manufacturer and follow suggested guidelines. Never refill a space heater while it is operating or still hot. Refuel heaters only outdoors.

Make sure wood stoves are properly installed, and at least 3 feet away from combustible materials. Ensure that they have the proper floor support and adequate ventilation. Use a glass or metal screen in front of your fireplace to prevent sparks from igniting nearby carpets, furniture, or other combustible items.

AND REMEMBER...

Be careful when using candles. Keep the flame away from combustible objects and out of the reach of children. Some smoke alarms may be dependent on your home's electrical service and could be inoperative during a power outage. Check to see if your smoke alarm uses a back-up battery and install a new battery at least once a year. Smoke alarms should be installed on every level of your home. All smoke alarms should be tested monthly. All batteries should be replaced with new ones at least once a year. If there is a fire hydrant near your home, keep it clear of debris for easy access by the fire department.

Summer Storms

SOME TYPES OF FIRE RELATED HAZARDS PRESENT DURING AND AFTER A SUMMER STORM

Lightning associated with thunderstorms generates a variety of fire hazards. The power of lightning's electrical charge and intense heat can electrocute on contact, splitting trees and causing fires. Pools of water and even appliances can be electrically charged. Appliances that have been exposed to water can short and become a fire hazard. Generators are often used during power outages. Generators that are not properly used and maintained can be very hazardous.

CHEMICAL SAFETY. Look for combustible liquids like gasoline, lighter fluid, and paint thinner that may have spilled. Thoroughly clean the spill and place containers in a well-ventilated area. Keep combustible liquids away from heat sources.

ELECTRICAL SAFETY. If your home has sustained flood or water damage, and you can safely get to the main breaker or fuse box, turn off the power. Assume all wires on the ground are electrically charged. This includes cable TV feeds. Be aware of and avoid downed utility lines. Report downed or damaged power lines to the utility company or emergency services. Remove standing water, wet carpets, and fur-nishings. Air dry your home with good ventilation before restoring power. Have a licensed electrician check your home for damage.

GAS SAFETY.   Smell and listen for leaky gas connections. If you believe there is a gas leak, immediately leave the house and leave the door(s) open. Never strike a match. Any size flame can spark an explosion. Before turning the gas back on, have the gas system checked by a professional.

GENERATOR SAFETY.   Follow the manufacturer's instructions and guidelines when using generators. Use a generator or other fuel-powered machines outside the home. Carbon monoxide fumes are odorless and can quickly overwhelm you indoors. Use the appropriate sized and type power cords to carry the electric load. Overloaded cords can overheat and cause fires. Never run cords under rugs or carpets where heat might build up or damage to a cord may go unnoticed. Never connect generators to another power source such as power lines. The reverse flow of electricity or "backfeed" can electrocute an unsuspecting utility worker.

HEATING SAFETY.   Kerosene heaters may not be legal in your area and should only be used where approved by authorities. Do not use the kitchen oven range to heat your home. In addition to being a fire hazard, it can be a source of toxic fumes. Alternative heaters need their space. Keep anything combustible at least 3 feet away. Make sure your alternative heaters have "tip switches." These "tip switches" are designed to automatically turn off the heater in the event they tip over. Only use the type of fuel recommended by the manufacturer and follow suggested guidelines. Never refill a space heater while it is operating or still hot. Refuel heaters only outdoors.

Make sure wood stoves are properly installed, and at least 3 feet away from combustible materials. Ensure that they have the proper floor support and adequate ventilation. Use a glass or metal screen in front of your fireplace to prevent sparks from igniting nearby carpets, furniture, or other combustible items.

AND REMEMBER...

Be careful when using candles. Keep the flame away from combustible objects and out of the reach of children. Some smoke alarms may be dependent on your home's electrical service and could be inoperative during a power outage. Check to see if your smoke alarm uses a back-up battery and install a new battery at least once a year. Smoke alarms should be installed on every level of your home. All smoke alarms should be tested monthly. All batteries should be replaced with new ones at least once a year. If there is a fire hydrant near your home, keep it clear of debris for easy access by the fire department.

REFERENCE #19
YOUR FAMILY DISASTER PLAN

Disaster can strike quickly and without warning. It can force you to evacuate your neighborhood or confine you to your home. What would you do if basic services—water, gas, electricity, or telephones— were cut off? Local officials and relief workers will be on the scene after a disaster, but they cannot reach everyone right away.

Families can—and do—cope with disaster by preparing in advance and working together as a team. Follow the steps listed here to create your family's disaster plan. Knowing what to do is your best protection and your responsibility.

Where will your family be when disaster strikes? They could be anywhere—at work, at school, or in the car. How will you find each other? Will you know if your children are safe?

4 Steps to Safety

1. FIND OUT WHAT COULD HAPPEN TO YOU

- Contact your local emergency management or civil defense office and American Red Cross chapter—be prepared to take notes.
- Ask what types of disasters are most likely to happen. Request information on how to prepare for each.
- Learn about your community's warning signals: what they sound like and what you should do when you hear them.
- Ask about animal care after disaster. Animals may not be allowed inside emergency shelters due to health regulations.
- Find out how to help elderly or disabled persons, if needed.
- Next, find out about the disaster plans at your workplace, your children's school or daycare center, and other places where your family spends time.

2. CREATE A DISASTER PLAN

- Meet with your family and discuss why you need to prepare for disaster. Explain the dangers of fire, severe weather, and earthquakes to children. Plan to share responsibilities and work together as a team.
- Discuss the types of disasters that are most likely to happen. Explain what to do in each case.
- Pick two places to meet:
  1. Right outside your home in case of a sudden emergency, like a fire.
  2. Outside your neighborhood in case you can't return home. Everyone must know the address and phone number. Ask an out-of-state friend to be your "family contact." After a disaster, its often easier to call long distance. Other family members should call this person and tell them where they are. Everyone must know your contact's phone number. Discuss what to do in an evacuation. Plan how to take care of your pets.

3. COMPLETE THIS CHECKLIST·

- Post emergency telephone numbers by phones (fire, police, ambulance, etc.).
- Teach children how and when to call 9-1-1 or your local Emergency Medical Services number for emergency help.
- Show each family member how and when to turn off the water, gas, and electricity at the main switches.
- Make sure that you have adequate insurance coverage.
- Teach each family member how to use the fire extinguisher (ABC type), and show them where it's kept.
- Install smoke detectors on each level of your home, especially near bedrooms.
- Conduct a home hazard hunt.
- Stock emergency supplies and assemble a Disaster Supplies Kit.
- Take a Red Cross first aid and CPR class.
- Determine the best escape routes from your home. Find two ways out of each room.
- Find the safe spots in your home for each type of disaster.

4. PRACTICE AND MAINTAIN YOUR PLAN

- Quiz your kids every six months so they remember what to do.
- Conduct fire and emergency evacuation drills.
- Replace stored water every three months and stored food every six months.
- Test and recharge your fire extinguisher(s) according to manufacturer's instructions.
- Test your smoke detectors monthly and change the batteries at least once a year.

Emergency Supplies

Keep enough supplies in your home to meet your needs for at least three days. Assemble a Disaster Supplies Kit with items you may need in an evacuation. Store these supplies in sturdy, easy-to-carry containers such as backpacks, duffel bags, or covered trash containers.

Include:

- A three-day supply of water (one gallon per person per day) and food that won't spoil.
- One change of clothing and footwear per person, and one blanket or sleeping bag per person.
- A first aid kit that includes your family's prescription medications.
- Emergency tools including a battery-powered radio, flashlight, and plenty of extra batteries.
- An extra set of car keys and a credit card, cash, or traveler's checks.
- Sanitation supplies.
- Special items for infants, elderly, or disabled family members.
- An extra pair of eyeglasses.
- Keep important family documents in a waterproof container.
- Keep a smaller kit in the trunk of your car.

Utilities

- Locate the main electric fuse box, water service main, and natural gas main.
- Learn how and when to turn these utilities off. Teach all responsible family members. Keep necessary tools near gas and water shut-off valves.

- Remember, turn off the utilities only if you suspect the lines are damaged or if you are instructed to do so. If you turn the gas off, you will need a professional to turn it back on.

Neighbors Helping Neighbors

Working with neighbors can save lives and property. Meet with your neighbors to plan how the neighborhood could work together after a disaster until help arrives. If you're a member of a neighborhood organization, such as a home association or crime watch group, introduce disaster preparedness as a new activity. Know your neighbors' special skills (e.g., medical, technical) and consider how you could help neighbors who have special needs, such as disabled and elderly persons. Make plans for child care in case parents can't get home.

Home Hazard Hunt

During a disaster, ordinary objects in your home can cause injury or damage. Anything that can move, fall, break, or cause a fire is a home hazard. For example, a hot water heater or a bookshelf can fall. Inspect your home at least once a year and fix potential hazards.

Contact your local fire department to learn about home fire hazards.

Evacuation

- Evacuate immediately if told to do so.
- Listen to your battery-powered radio and follow the instructions of local emergency officials.
- Wear protective clothing and sturdy shoes.
- Take your family disaster supplies kit.
- Lock your home.
- Use travel routes specified by local authorities—don't use shortcuts because certain areas may be impassable or dangerous.
- If you're sure you have time:
  - Shut off water, gas, and electricity before leaving, if instructed to do so.

- Post a note telling others when you left and where you are going.
- Make arrangements for your pets.

If Disaster Strikes

- Remain calm and patient. Put your plan into action.
- Check for injuries.
- Give first aid and get help for seriously injured people.
- Listen to your battery-powered radio for news and instructions.
- Evacuate, if advised to do so. Wear protective clothing and sturdy shoes.
- Check for damage in your home:
  - Use flashlights—do not light matches or turn on electrical switches, if you suspect damage.
  - Check for fires, fire hazards, and other household hazards.
  - Sniff for gas leaks, starting at the water heater. If you smell gas or suspect a leak, turn off the main gas valve, open windows, and get everyone outside quickly.
  - Shut off any other damaged utilities.
  - Clean up spilled medicines, bleaches, gasoline, and other flammable liquids immediately.

REMEMBER TO:

- Confine or secure your pets.
- Call your family contact—do not use the telephone again unless it is a life-threatening emergency.
- Check on your neighbors, especially elderly or disabled persons.
- Make sure you have an adequate water supply in case service is cut off.
- Stay away from downed power lines.

The Federal Emergency Management Agency's Family Protection Program and the American Red Cross' Disaster Education Program are nationwide efforts to help citizens prepare for disasters of all types. For more information, please contact your local emergency management or civil defense office, and your local American Red Cross chapter. Start planning now.

Request free family protection publications by writing to:
FEMA
P.O. Box 70274
Washington, DC 20024
Ask for: "Are You Ready?,"
"Your Family Disaster Supplies Kit," and
"Emergency Food and Water Supplies."

REFERENCE #20
YOUR FAMILY DISASTER
SUPPLIES KIT

After a disaster, local officials and relief workers will be on the scene, but they cannot reach everyone immediately. You could get help in hours, or it may take days. Would your family be prepared to cope with the emergency until help arrives?

Your family will cope best by preparing for disaster before it strikes. One way to prepare is by assembling a Disaster Supplies Kit. Once disaster hits, you won't have time to shop or search for supplies. But if you've gathered supplies in advance, your family can endure an evacuation or home confinement.

To prepare your kit:

- Review the checklists in this section. Gather the supplies that are listed. You may need them if your family is confined at home.
- Place the supplies you'd most likely need for an evacuation in an easy-to-carry container. These supplies are listed with an asterisk (*).
- Disasters happen any time and anywhere. And when disaster strikes, you may not have much time to respond.
- A highway spill of hazardous material could mean instant evacuation.
- A winter storm could confine your family at home. An earthquake, flood, tornado, or any other disaster could cut off basic services—gas, water, electricity, and telephones—for days.

Water

Store water in plastic containers such as soft drink bottles. Avoid using containers that will decompose or break, such as milk cartons or glass bottles. A normally active person needs to drink at least two quarts of water each day. Hot environments and intense physical activity can double that amount. Children, nursing mothers, and ill people will need more.

Store one gallon of water per person per day (two quarts for drinking, two quarts for food preparation/sanitation).*

Keep at least a three-day supply of water for each person in your household.

Food

Store at least a three-day supply of non-perishable food. Select foods that require no refrigeration, preparation, or cooking and little or no water. If you must heat food, pack a can of Sterno. Select food items that are compact and lightweight.

Include a selection of the following foods in your Disaster Supplies Kit:*

- Ready-to-eat canned meats, fruits, and vegetables
- Canned juices, milk, soup (if powdered, store extra water)
- Staples—sugar, salt, pepper
- High-energy foods—peanut butter, jelly, crackers, granola bars, trail mix
- Vitamins
- Foods for infants, elderly persons, or persons on special diets
- Comfort/stress foods—cookies, hard candy, sweetened cereals, lollipops, instant coffee, tea bags

First Aid Kit

Assemble a first aid kit for your home and one for each car. A first aid kit* should include:
Sterile adhesive bandages in assorted sizes
2-inch sterile gauze pads (4–6)
4-inch sterile gauze pads (4–6)
Hypoallergenic adhesive tape
Triangular bandages (3)
2-inch sterile roller bandages (3 rolls)
3-inch sterile roller bandages (3 rolls)
Scissors
Tweezers
Needle
Moistened towelettes
Antiseptic

Thermometer
Tongue blades (2)
Tube of petroleum jelly or other lubricant
Assorted sizes of safety pins
Cleansing agent/soap
Latex gloves (2 pair)
Sunscreen

NON-PRESCRIPTION DRUGS

Aspirin or non-aspirin pain reliever
Anti-diarrhea medication
Antacid (for stomach upset)
Syrup of Ipecac (use to induce vomiting if advised by the Poison
    Control Center)
Laxatives
Activated charcoal (use if advised by the Poison Control Center)

Contact your local American Red Cross chapter to obtain a basic
first aid manual.

Supplies

There are six basics you should stock in your home: water, food, first
aid supplies, clothing and bedding, tools, and emergency supplies and
special items. Keep the items that you would most likely need during
an evacuation in an easy-to-carry container—suggested items are
marked with an asterisk (*). Possible containers include a large, covered trash container, a camping backpack, or a duffel bag.

TOOLS AND SUPPLIES

Mess kits, or paper cups, plates, and plastic utensils*
Emergency preparedness manual*
Battery-operated radio and extra batteries*
Flashlight and extra batteries*
Cash or traveler's checks, change*
Nonelectric can opener, utility knife*

Fire extinguisher: small canister, ABC type
Tube tent
Pliers
Tape
Compass
Matches in a waterproof container
Aluminum foil
Plastic storage containers
Signal flare
Paper, pencil
Needles, thread
Medicine dropper
Shut-off wrench, to turn off household gas and water
Whistle
Plastic sheeting
Map of the area (for locating shelters)

SANITATION

Toilet paper, towelettes*
Soap, liquid detergent*
Feminine supplies*
Personal hygiene items*
Plastic garbage bags, ties (for personal sanitation uses)
Plastic bucket with tight lid
Disinfectant
Household chlorine bleach

CLOTHING AND BEDDING (INCLUDE AT LEAST ONE COMPLETE CHANGE OF CLOTHING AND FOOTWEAR PER PERSON.*)

Sturdy shoes or work boots*
Hat and gloves
Rain gear*
Thermal underwear
Blankets or sleeping bags*
Sunglasses

SPECIAL ITEMS (REMEMBER FAMILY MEMBERS WITH SPECIAL NEEDS, SUCH AS INFANTS AND ELDERLY OR DISABLED PERSONS.)

*For Baby**
Formula
Diapers
Bottles
Powdered milk
Medications
*For Adults**
Heart and high blood pressure medication
Insulin
Prescription drugs
Denture needs
Contact lenses and supplies
Extra eye glasses
Entertainment—games and books.

IMPORTANT FAMILY DOCUMENTS (KEEP THESE RECORDS IN A WATERPROOF, PORTABLE CONTAINER.)

Will, insurance policies, contracts, deeds, stocks and bonds
Passports, social security cards, immunization records
Bank account numbers
Credit card account numbers and companies
Inventory of valuable household goods, important telephone numbers
Family records (birth, marriage, death certificates)

Suggestions and Reminders

- Store your kit in a convenient place known to all family members.
- Keep a smaller version of the Disaster Supplies Kit in the trunk of your car.
- Keep items in air-tight plastic bags.
- Change your stored water supply every 3 months so it stays fresh.
- Rotate your stored food every six months.

- Rethink your kit and family needs at least once a year. Replace batteries, update clothes, etc.
- Ask your physician or pharmacist about storing prescription medications.

Create a Family Disaster Plan

TO GET STARTED...

- Contact your local emergency management or civil defense office and your local American Red Cross chapter.
- Find out which disasters are most likely to happen in your community.
- Ask how you would be warned.
- Find out how to prepare for each.
- Meet with your family.
- Discuss the types of disasters that could occur.
- Explain how to prepare and respond.
- Discuss what to do if advised to evacuate.
- Practice what you have discussed.
- Plan how your family will stay in contact if separated by disaster.
- Pick two meeting places:
  1. a location a safe distance from your home in case of fire.
  2. a place outside your neighborhood in case you can't return home. Choose an out-of-state friend as a "check-in contact" for everyone to call.
- Complete these steps:
  1. Post emergency telephone numbers by every phone.
  2. Show responsible family members how and when to shut off water, gas, and electricity at main switches.
  3. Install a smoke detector on each level of your home, especially near bedrooms; test monthly and change the batteries two times each year.
  4. Contact your local fire department to learn about home fire hazards.
  5. Learn first aid and CPR. Contact your local American Red Cross chapter for information and training.
- Meet with your neighbors.

Know your neighbors' skills (medical, technical). Consider how you could help neighbors who have special needs, such as elderly or disabled persons.

Make plans for child care in case parents can't get home.

Remember to practice and maintain your plan.

Preparedness Program and the American Red Cross Disaster Education Program are nationwide efforts to help people prepare for disasters of all types. For more information, please contact your local or State Office of Emergency Management, and your local American Red Cross chapter.

Ask for "Your Family Disaster Plan" and the "Emergency Preparedness Checklist."

Or write to: FEMA P.O. Box 70274 Washington, D.C. 20024

REFERENCE #21
DISASTERS AND PEOPLE
WITH DISABILITIES

This book has been designed to show the "average" person how to live as normally as possible after any disaster that interrupts the infrastructure. However, in addition to the "average" person, people with disabilities may need to make special preparations. This chapter contains information from both FEMA and The Red Cross. For more information contact them or visit their Web sites at:

FEMA (Federal Emergency Management Agency): www.fema.gov

The American Red Cross: www.redcross.org

People With Disabilities
(From FEMA)

- Maintain a list of the following important items and store it with the emergency supplies. Give a copy to another family member and a friend or neighbor.
  - Special equipment and supplies, e.g., hearing aid batteries
  - Current prescriptions names and dosages
  - Names, addresses, and telephone numbers of doctors and pharmacist
  - Detailed information about the specifications of your medication regime
  - Create a self-help network of relatives, friends, or co-workers to assist in an emergency
- If you think you may need assistance in a disaster, discuss your disability with relatives, friends, and co-workers and ask for their help. For example, if you need help moving or require special arrangements to receive emergency messages, make a plan with friends. Make sure they know where you keep emergency supplies. Give a key to a neighbor or friend who may be able to assist you in a disaster.

- Contact your local emergency information management office now. Many local emergency management offices maintain registers of people with disabilities so they can be located and assisted quickly in a disaster.
- Wearing medical alert tags or bracelets to identify your disability may help in case of an emergency.
- Know the location and availability of more than one facility if you are dependent on a dialysis machine or other life-sustaining equipment or treatment.
- If you have a severe speech, language, or hearing disability:
  - When you dial 9-1-1, tap space bar to indicate TDD call.
  - Store a writing pad and pencils to communicate with others.
  - Keep a flashlight handy to signal whereabouts to other people and for illumination to aid in communication.
  - Remind friends that you cannot completely hear warnings or emergency instructions. Ask them to be your source of emergency information as it comes over their radio.
  - If you have a hearing ear dog, be aware that the dog may become confused or disoriented in an emergency. Store extra food, water, and supplies for your dog.

PLANNING FOR EVACUATION

People with disabilities have the same choices as other community residents about whether to evacuate their homes and where to go when an emergency threatens. Listen to the advice of local officials. Decide whether it is better to leave the area, stay with a friend, or go to a public shelter. Each of these decisions requires planning and preparation.

If you need a wheelchair:

- Show friends how to operate your wheelchair so they can move you if necessary.
- Make sure your friends know the size of your wheelchair in case it has to be transported.

Creating a Personal Support Network
(From The American Red Cross)

A personal support network (sometimes called a self-help team, but referred to only as a "network" in this book) can help you prepare for a disaster. It can do this by helping you identify and get the resources you need to cope effectively with a disaster. Your network can help you practice vital activities, like evaluating your home or workplace. Network members can also assist you after a disaster happens. You should put together your network before you assess what your needs will be during and after a disaster.

Organize a network for your home, school, workplace, volunteer site, and any other place where you spend a lot of time. Members of your network can be roommates, relatives, neighbors, friends, and co-workers. They should be people you trust and who could check to see if you need assistance. They should know your capabilities and needs, and offer help within minutes.

Do not depend on only one person. Include a minimum of three people in your network for each location where you regularly spend a lot of time during the week.

Think of what your needs would be during a disaster and discuss these with each of your networks. Complete a written assessment of your needs with your network in the space provided in the following section. This can help your network members learn the best ways to assist you and offer additional ideas for you to think about.

Give your network members copies of your emergency information list, medical information list, disability-related supplies and special equipment list, evacuation plans, relevant emergency documents, and personal disaster plan when you complete them.

Your network should know your capabilities and needs and offer help within minutes.

Arrange with your network to check on you immediately if local officials give an evacuation order or if a disaster occurs. Do this before an emergency happens so that your network members can help you when you need them. Also, ask your network to notify you of an emergency you may not know about. For example, if a siren or loud speaker system notifies a neighborhood of a disaster and you are Deaf or have hearing loss, be sure that your network knows to give you this information. Ask them to give you any other disaster-related information that is not already in writing, such as radio information about the disaster or the location of shelters.

Agree on how you and your network will contact each other during an emergency. Do not count on the telephones working. Also, choose a signal for help that you both understand. Signals can be shouting, knocking on the wall, or using a whistle, bell, or high-pitched noisemaker. Visual signals could include hanging a sheet outside your window.

Give the members of your network all the necessary keys they may need to get into your home, car, etc. Show your network how to operate and safely move the equipment you use for your disability, if necessary. Ask them to "practice" with any of your special equipment. This will help them feel more comfortable when using it during an emergency.

Make sure your service animal knows the people in your network. This will make it easier for the animal to accept care from someone other than yourself.

Explain to your network any assistance for personal care that you may need. Give them written instructions on how best to assist you and your animals.

Label your equipment and attach instruction cards on how to use and move each item. Laminate the instruction cards for added durability.

Inform your network about any areas on your body where you have reduced feeling. Have them check these areas for injuries after a disaster if you cannot check them yourself.

Practice your plan. Based on your knowledge of the disasters in your area, simulate any problems or obstacles you may experience. Have the members of your network practice how to help you, and familiarize them with any adaptive equipment you may need.

Choose an emergency meeting place you are familiar with where you and others can reunite after exiting a building. You should select a meeting place for each area where you spend a lot of time.

Select with your network a signal that you can use to let them know you are okay and have left the site.

Give your network your travel dates if you will be traveling.

Review and revise your personal assessment and disaster plan regularly, or as your condition changes. Your network should help in this review as well. You will also find that as you and your network practice, all of you will find problems and solutions you have not thought of before.

The trusting relationship you develop with the members of your network should be mutual. Learn about each other's needs and how to assist each other during an emergency.

© Copyright 1998, The American National Red Cross. All Rights Reserved.

Personal Disaster Preparation
(From The American Red Cross)

How well you prepare and how much you practice before a disaster occurs will determine how successfully you deal with and recover from disasters. Your personal disaster preparation is a continuing process. It helps you and your network identify, obtain, develop, manage, and maintain the information and resources you will need to deal with a disaster when it happens.

Prepare yourself based on the capabilities and limitations you believe you will have after the disaster. Also keep in mind that your usual ways of support and assistance may not be available to you for some time during an evacuation and after the disaster has occurred.

Make a personal disaster plan. This will help you organize information you will need and activities you will do during and after a disaster. Key items in a personal disaster plan are described below. Keep copies of your disaster plan in your disaster supplies kit, car, wallet (behind driver's license or primary identification card), wheelchair pack, or at work, etc. Also, share your disaster plan with your network.

EMERGENCY INFORMATION LIST

Make an emergency information list that you and your network can use. This list will let others know whom to call if they find you unconscious, unable to speak, or if they need to help you evacuate quickly. Besides emergency out-of-town contacts, your list should include the names and numbers of everyone in your network.

Ask a relative or friend who lives more than 100 miles away from you to be your "contact person. " Keep in mind that a caller is more likely to connect with a long-distance number outside the disaster area than with a local number within it. In fact, all family members in a disaster area should call the contact person and give their location and condition. Once this is done, have the contact person give messages to your other friends and relatives who live outside the disaster area.

This will help reduce calling into and out of the affected area once the phones are working.

If you have a communication disability, make sure your emergency information list notes the best way to communicate with you. This may be by writing notes, pointing to letters, words, or pictures, or finding a quiet place.

MEDICAL INFORMATION LIST

Complete a medical information list that you and your network can use. The list should have information about your medical providers. Also include the names of medications you take and their dosages, when you take a medication, the condition for which you take a medication, the name of the doctor who prescribed it, and the doctor's phone number. It is important to record any adaptive equipment you use, your allergies and sensitivities, and communication or cognitive difficulties you may have. Keep this list attached to your emergency information list (described above).

Attach copies of health insurance cards and related information to the medical information list. Keep at least a seven-day supply of essential medications with you at all times. Work with your doctor(s) to get extra supplies of medications and extra copies of prescriptions. Talk with your doctor or pharmacist about what you should do if you do not have enough medicine after a disaster and cannot immediately get what you need. Be sure you ask about the shelf life of your medications and the temperatures at which they should be stored. Determine how often you should replace stored medication. This helps ensure that a medicine's effectiveness does not weaken because of long storage time.

Note: If you take medications (such as methadone, chemotherapy, or radiation therapy) administered to you by a clinic or hospital, ask your provider how you should prepare for a disruption caused by a disaster.

WHAT YOU CAN DO TO PREPARE FOR A DISASTER

Earthquake:

Identify a sturdy table or desk to get under in each room. This is important because while the earth is shaking, the movement of the ground will probably make it difficult or impossible for you to move any distance. If you cannot safely get under a desk or table, move near an inside wall of the building and cover your head and neck as best you can. Decide how you will get there when the earthquake begins. Lock your wheels if you are in a wheelchair. In bed, pull the sheets and blankets over you and use your pillow to cover and protect your head and neck.

Tornado:

The lowest floor or below-ground area of your home or workplace is safest. If there is no basement or you cannot get there, choose a room without windows, such as a bathroom or closet. Identify where this safe place is and how you would get there.

Hurricane or flood:

If local officials have not told you to leave the area, stay upstairs and in the middle of the building, away from windows. Avoid going to the lowest floor because hurricanes often cause flooding. If you are blind or visually impaired, use a long cane in areas where debris may have fallen or furniture may have shifted. This is recommended even if you do not usually use a cane indoors. For information about how to prepare for disasters that are specific to your area, contact your local Red Cross chapter.

Keep your service animals with you in a safe place at home, or take them with you to a shelter. Install at least one smoke detector on each level of your home, outside sleeping areas. If you are deaf or have hearing loss, install a system that has flashing strobe lights to get your attention. If you have battery-operated detectors, replace batteries at least once a year, such as on your birthday, New Year's Day, etc. Test smoke detectors once a month by pushing the test button. Find the location of main utility cutoff valves and switches in your home. Learn how and when to disconnect them during an emergency. Try to do this yourself (do not practice shutting off the gas). If you cannot practice alone, arrange for your network to help. Turn off utilities only if local officials tell you to do so or if you believe there is an immediate threat to life. For example, if you smell gas, see or hear sparking wires, or see water gushing from broken pipes, you should turn off utilities immediately. If you turn gas off, only a professional should turn it back on. If you cannot use the proper tools to turn utilities off at the main valves or switches, turn off the valves under sinks and by the stove. Also, turn off all electrical switches in every room. Be sure that the members of your network know the following information:

- Where to find each utility shutoff valve.
- How to turn off each utility.
- Whether you have the proper tools and where they are located, or if your network members need to bring tools with them.

Identify as many exits as possible from each room and from the building you are in. Be sure to include the windows as exits. Make a floor plan of your home. You may want your network to assist you with it. Include your primary escape routes. On the floor plan, mark the rooms where you spend a lot of time. Also, mark where your disaster supplies kit is located. Give a copy of the floor plan to your network. This will help them find you and your supplies, if necessary. When traveling, know the types of disasters that threaten the area you will be visiting. Let the hotel or motel front desk know of your possible needs in case of an emergency. Describe the type of help you may need. Remember to let your network members know your travel plans: when you will leave and when you will return.

PREPARE AN EVACUATION PLAN BEFORE A DISASTER HAPPENS

If you have to leave your home or workplace, you may need someone's help to evacuate safely, especially down stairwells. If you need assistance during an emergency and your network is not available, find helpers and tell them about your condition. Give them instructions on what you need and how they can help you evacuate.

Practice using different ways out of a building, especially if you are above the first floor in a building with many stories. Remember, the elevator may not work or should not be used. Decide what type of equipment you may need for assistance during an evacuation. If you cannot use stairs, talk with your network about how you should be evacuated. They may want to take the Red Cross First Responder course or other to avoid injuring you or themselves.

If you need devices for an emergency escape, make a purchase. Store devices nearby, where you can get to them easily. This may mean having more than one emergency escape device available.

Be an advocate for yourself. Practice how to quickly explain to people the best way to guide or move you and your adaptive equipment, safely and rapidly.

Be ready to give brief, clear, and specific instructions and directions to rescue personnel, either orally or in writing. For example, say or write these instructions:

"Please take my—
Oxygen tank.
Wheelchair.
Gamma globulin from the freezer.
Insulin from the refrigerator.
Communication device from under the bed."

"Please do not straighten my knees. They are fused in a bent position."
"I have had a brain injury. Please write down all important instructions and information."
"I am blind/visually impaired. Please let me grasp your arm firmly."
"I am deaf. Please write things down for me."

When needed, ask for an accommodation from disaster response personnel. For example, let a responder or relief worker know if you cannot wait in lines for long periods for items like water, food, and disaster relief assistance.

Practice how to explain clearly and briefly why you need this assistance. You may also want to write the explanation down ahead of time.

Keep your automobile fuel tank more than half full at all times. Also, stock your vehicle with a small disaster supplies kit. If you do not drive, talk with your network about how you will leave the area if the authorities advise an evacuation. In some communities, local government agencies offer transportation for persons needing assistance during an evacuation. Ask your local emergency management office if these services are available in your area for persons with your disability.

Become familiar with the emergency or disaster/evacuation plan for your office, school, or any other location where you spend a lot of time. If the current plan does not make arrangements for people with disabilities, make sure the management at these sites knows your needs. Be sure that you are included in the overall plan for safety and evacuation of the building.

Choose an alternate place to stay, such as with friends, family, or at a hotel or motel outside your area if you have been told to leave your home. You may have enough early warning time (as with a slow-rising flood or hurricane) to leave before the disaster occurs. This is especially important if you live in a mobile home or trailer. Find out if there are predesignated shelters in your area and where they are.

Have a care plan for your pet. Plan for the care of your pets if you have to evacuate your home. Pets, unlike service animals, will not be allowed into emergency shelters. So, it is best to decide now where you will take your pet if you must leave. Contact your local Red Cross chapter or Humane Society for more information.

Have a care plan for your service animal. Service animals are allowed in hotels or motels and Red Cross shelters. However, these places cannot care for your animal. When you leave your home, remember to take a collar, harness, identification tags, records of vaccinations, medications, and food for your service animal with you.

Summary Checklist for Personal Disaster Preparation

There are many parts to a personal disaster plan. Fortunately, they do not have to be completed all at once. As you finish each part of your preparation, note the date in the space provided below. Review and update this plan regularly.

Date Completed_____

❏ Make an emergency information list.
Include:
Medical and emergency contact information.
Emergency out-of-town contacts.
Names and numbers of everyone in your network.
Name and number of a relative or friend who lives more than 100 miles away from you.

If you have a communication disability, make sure your emergency information list notes the best way to communicate with you.

❑ Fill out a medical information list.
  Include information about:
    Medical providers
    Medications you use
    Adaptive equipment and/or body system support equipment you use
    Allergies and sensitivities
    Communication or cognitive difficulties

❑ Attach copies of health insurance cards and related information to your medical information list.

❑ Keep at least a seven-day supply of essential medications with you at all times.

❑ Have extra copies of prescriptions.

❑ Talk with your doctor or pharmacist about what you should do if you do not have enough medicine after a disaster. Also, find out the shelf life of your medication and the storage temperature it needs. Determine how often you should replace stored medication.

❑ Identify safe places to go to during an—
    Earthquake
    Tornado
    Hurricane
    Flood
    Fire

❑ Install at least one smoke detector on each level of your home, outside sleeping areas.

❑ Find the location of utility cutoff valves and switches. Become familiar with how to operate them.

❑ Identify as many exits as possible (but at least two) from each room and from the building you are in.

❑ Make a floor plan of your home. You may want your network to help you do this. Include your primary escape routes.

❑ Practice using different ways out of a building, especially if you are above the first floor in a building with many stories.

❑ Decide what type of equipment you will need for assistance during an evacuation.

❑ Be ready to give brief, clear, specific instructions and directions to rescue personnel.

❑ If you do not drive, talk with your network about how you will leave the area if authorities advise an evacuation.

❑ Ask your local emergency management office if transportation services are available to persons with your disability during an emergency evacuation. Find out how to arrange to get this service.

❑ Become familiar with the emergency or disaster evacuation plan for your office, school, or any other location where you spend a lot of time.

❑ Choose an alternate place to stay.

❑ Have a care plan for your pet.

❑ Have a care plan for your service animal.

© Copyright 1998, The American National Red Cross. All Rights Reserved.

Disaster Supplies

(From The American Red Cross)

DISABILITY-RELATED SUPPLIES AND SPECIAL EQUIPMENT

Your disability-related supplies can be part of both your basic and your portable disaster supplies kit.

List the special supplies and equipment you may need. Be sure to note the places where they are stored.

Keep mobility aids near you at all times. If you have extra aids (such as a cane), have them available in several locations.

Disability-related supplies can be part of both your basic and your portable disaster supplies kits. If you must leave your home for any reason, your disability-related supplies will be available to take with you. If you are confined to your home, these supplies will be available along with your basic disaster supplies kit.

PORTABLE DISASTER SUPPLIES KIT

Know where your disaster supply kit is at all times.

Get a drawstring bag, a pouch with lots of pockets, a fanny pack, or a small backpack and keep it within reach, by or on your chair, wheelchair, scooter, or other assistive device.

Your portable disaster supplies kit should include a copy of your emergency information list and other lists; a small flashlight; a whistle or noisemaker; water; extra medication and copies of prescriptions; an extra pair of glasses; a hearing aid; sanitary supplies; a pad and pencil or other writing device; and a pair of heavy work gloves for wheeling over glass and debris.

At night, keep these portable supplies either next to or under your bed.

DISASTER SUPPLIES FOR YOUR CAR

Store basic disaster supplies and other emergency items in your car.

Besides the basic disaster supplies, you should also carry other disaster supplies in your car. Store several blankets; an extra set of mittens or gloves, wool socks, and a wool cap; jumper cables and instructions; a small sack of sand or kitty litter for traction; a small shovel; a set of tire chains or traction mats; a red cloth to use as a flag; and a CB radio or cellular telephone in any vehicle you use regularly.

POWER-DEPENDENT EQUIPMENT

Some people may use a fuel-operated generator to produce electricity if power will be out for a long time. If appropriate and feasible, get a generator listed by Underwriters Laboratories (the generator will carry a label with the letters "UL" circled on it).

Some generators can be connected to the existing wiring systems of a house. But contact your utility company before you connect a generator to house wiring. Connecting a generator is specifically prohibited by law in some areas, so you must check with your local utility or fire department first.

To run generators in an emergency, fuel must be safely stored. Generators need to be operated outdoors to guarantee good ventilation. If you get a generator, be sure your network is familiar with how to operate it.

If you use a battery-operated wheelchair, life-support system, or other power-dependent equipment, discuss with your power company the type of backup power you plan to use.

Some utility companies offer a "priority reconnection service" for people with disabilities who use power-dependent equipment. Many utility companies keep a list and map of the locations of power-dependent customers in case of an emergency.

Contact the customer service department of your local utility company(ies) to learn if this service is available in your community. Some utility companies may require a referral from your physician to qualify you for this service. However, even with this "priority reconnection service," your power could still be out for a long time following a disaster. Providing alternatives for your power-dependent equipment is still essential.

ADDITIONAL INFORMATION ON EQUIPMENT AND SUPPLIES

If you use a wheelchair or scooter:

- Keep a patch kit and can of seal-in-air product in your portable disaster supplies kit to repair flat tires, unless these are puncture-proof. Also, keep an extra supply of inner tubes.
- Keep a pair of heavy gloves in your portable disaster supplies kit to use while wheeling or making your way over glass and debris.
- In areas prone to earthquakes, keep the wheelchair wheels locked and the wheelchair close to your bed at night to be sure it does not move or fall over.

- Have an extra battery. A car battery also can be used with a wheelchair but will not last as long as a wheelchair's deep-cycle battery.
- Check with your vendor to know if you can charge your battery by either connecting jumper cables to a vehicle battery or connecting batteries to a converter that plugs into a vehicle's cigarette lighter. Caution: Charge only one battery at a time.
- If available, store a lightweight manual wheelchair for backup.

If you are blind or have a visual disability:

- Store a talking or braille clock or large-print timepiece with extra batteries.
- Have at least one extra white cane.
- Mark your disaster supplies items with fluorescent tape, large print, or braille.
- Mark your gas, water, and electric shutoff valves with fluorescent tape, large print, or braille.
- Store extra magnifiers.
- Have an extra pair of glasses if you wear them.
- Make photocopies of your information lists from this book.

If you are deaf or have a hearing loss:

- Consider getting a small portable battery-operated television set. Emergency broadcasts may give information in American Sign Language (ASL) or open captioning.
- Keep pads and pencils in your home disaster supplies kit and with your car disaster supplies. Keep them with you at all times for communication.
- Keep a flashlight, whistle, or other noisemaker, and pad and pencil by your bed.
- Keep a card in the disaster supplies kits (in your home and car), and with you at all times that indicates that you are deaf. Include any other appropriate communication "know American Sign Language (ASL)," or, "My service animal may legally remain with me."

If you have a speech-related or communication disability:

- Consider buying a power converter if you use a laptop computer to communicate. A power converter allows most laptops (12 volts or less) to be operated from the cigarette lighter on the dashboard of a vehicle.
- Be sure to have pencil and paper with you as a backup communication resource.
- If you use an augmentative communication device (such as an electronic communicator or artificial larynx) that allows you to communicate by voice, be sure to keep it close to you at night in a safe place.
- Store copies of a word or letter board and preprinted key phrases you would use in case of an emergency in all of your disaster supplies kits, your wallet, purse, etc.

If you use self-administered medical treatments:

- Keep in mind that traffic delays and/or severe weather hazards can happen when you do not expect them. Be sure to carry the equipment and fluids (temperature controlled) you will need when traveling.

If you have a cognitive disability:

- Keep a copy of any instructions or information you think you will need. Also, keep a copy of this information in the disaster supplies kits you keep both at home and in your car. Prepare this information in a way that is easy for you to understand. You may want to break down the information into a step-by-step outline. This format will help you remember what to do during the confusion of a disaster.
- Have a pencil and paper ready to keep track of any new instructions or information you may receive.

STORING SUPPLIES

Store emergency documents in sealed plastic freezer bags in your basic disaster supplies kit. Copies of lifesaving information (i.e., specifications for adaptive equipment or medical devices) should be stored in your basic disaster supplies kits and with your disability-related supplies, portable supplies kit, car supplies, and supplies you keep at work.

Keep other emergency documents in your disaster supplies kit at home so you can get to them in an emergency.

If you get benefits from Social Security (SSI or SSD), put a copy of your most recent award letter with these documents as well. (Note: financial assistance from the American Red Cross and other disaster recovery resources will not cause a reduction in your monthly grant.)

Be sure to send copies of these documents to your out-of-town contact person (seal and mark them "open in an emergency for [name] only").

Store your disaster supplies kit in a safe, dry place that is easy for you to get to. This place should also be easy for your network, or anyone who comes to assist you, to identify. If you are going to put the kit on a shelf, be sure to secure it so that it does not fall and become inaccessible when you need it.

Replace your supply of food and water every six months.

Also, check the expiration dates of stored prescription medications. Replace items in your supplies kit that are old or outdated. Remember to do this by putting new purchases in the kit and using the old kit items you purchased earlier. However, do not borrow items from the kit with the intention of replacing them later. You may forget to do so.

Summary Checklist for Disaster Supplies

❑ Put together a basic disaster supplies kit for your home. It should have food, water, and other essential items you would need for at least three, but preferably seven days.

❑ Obtain a first aid kit and put it with your basic disaster supplies kit for home.

❑ Collect items for a disaster supplies kit containing items you need that are related to your disability.

❑ Put together a portable disaster supplies kit in a drawstring bag or pouch to carry with you at all times.

❑ Assemble a disaster supplies kit for your car or van.

❏ Assemble disaster supplies for your service animal and pet(s).

❏ Obtain a UL-listed generator if you have equipment that runs on electricity and needs backup power.

❏ Ask your utility company if a priority reconnection service is available in your area.

❏ Get a patch kit and canned air for wheelchair tires.

❏ Put heavy gloves in your portable disaster supplies kit if you use a wheelchair. Wear these gloves when wheeling over debris.

❏ Keep an extra battery available for a motorized wheelchair.

© Copyright 1998, The American National Red Cross. All Rights Reserved.

Important Lists

EMERGENCY INFORMATION LIST

Please complete this form and distribute copies to your emergency contact people as well as to each member in your network.

Name: _____

Birth date: _____

Address: _____

Telephone number: _____

Social Security number: _____

Local emergency contact person: _____

Emergency contact person's numbers: _____

Network members: _____

Network members' home/work numbers: _____

Out-of-town contact: _____

Out-of-town contact's numbers: _____

How best to communicate with me: _____

MEDICAL INFORMATION LIST

Please complete this form and distribute copies to your emergency contact people as well as to each member in your network.

Primary physician: _____

Telephone number: _____

Address: _____

Hospital affiliation: _____

Type of health insurance: _____

Policy number: _____

Blood type: _____

Allergies and sensitivities: _____

Medications and dosages being taken: _____

Specific medical conditions: _____

Physical limitations: _____

Adaptive equipment and vendors' phones: _____

Communication difficulties: _____

Cognitive difficulties: _____

DISABILITY-RELATED SUPPLIES AND SPECIAL EQUIPMENT LIST

Check items you use, and describe item type and location. Distribute copies to your emergency contact people as well as to each member in your network.

❏ Glasses: _____

❏ Eating utensils: _____

❏ Grooming utensils: _____

❏ Dressing devices: _____

❏ Writing devices: _____

❏ Hearing device: _____

❑ Oxygen:_____
Flow rate: _____

❑ Suction equipment: _____

❑ Dialysis equipment: _____

❑ Sanitary supplies: _____

❑ Urinary supplies: _____

❑ Ostomy supplies: _____

❑ Wheelchair:_____
Wheelchair repair kit: _____
Motorized:_____
Manual: _____

❑ Walker: _____

❑ Crutches: _____

❑ Cane(s):_____

❑ Dentures:_____

❑ Monitors: _____

❑ Other: _____

INDEX

G

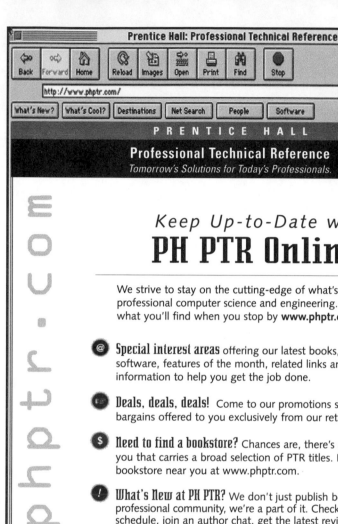

Prentice Hall: Professional Technical Reference

Back | Forward | Home | Reload | Images | Open | Print | Find | Stop

http://www.phptr.com/

What's New? | What's Cool? | Destinations | Net Search | People | Software

P R E N T I C E   H A L L

Professional Technical Reference
Tomorrow's Solutions for Today's Professionals.

Keep Up-to-Date with
PH PTR Online!

We strive to stay on the cutting-edge of what's happening in professional computer science and engineering. Here's a bit of what you'll find when you stop by **www.phptr.com**:

@ **Special interest areas** offering our latest books, book series, software, features of the month, related links and other useful information to help you get the job done.

Deals, deals, deals! Come to our promotions section for the latest bargains offered to you exclusively from our retailers.

$ **Need to find a bookstore?** Chances are, there's a bookseller near you that carries a broad selection of PTR titles. Locate a Magnet bookstore near you at www.phptr.com.

! **What's New at PH PTR?** We don't just publish books for the professional community, we're a part of it. Check out our convention schedule, join an author chat, get the latest reviews and press releases on topics of interest to you.

✉ **Subscribe Today!** **Join PH PTR's monthly email newsletter!**

Want to be kept up-to-date on your area of interest? Choose a targeted category on our website, and we'll keep you informed of the latest PH PTR products, author events, reviews and conferences in your interest area.

Visit our mailroom to subscribe today! **http://www.phptr.com/mail_lists**